T0311745

Cambridge Elements ≡

Elements in Philosophy and Logic
edited by
Bradley Armour-Garb
SUNY Albany
Frederick Kroon
The University of Auckland

SET THEORY

John P. Burgess
Princeton University

CAMBRIDGE
UNIVERSITY PRESS

CAMBRIDGE
UNIVERSITY PRESS

University Printing House, Cambridge CB2 8BS, United Kingdom

One Liberty Plaza, 20th Floor, New York, NY 10006, USA

477 Williamstown Road, Port Melbourne, VIC 3207, Australia

314–321, 3rd Floor, Plot 3, Splendor Forum, Jasola District Centre,
New Delhi – 110025, India

103 Penang Road, #05–06/07, Visioncrest Commercial, Singapore 238467

Cambridge University Press is part of the University of Cambridge.

It furthers the University's mission by disseminating knowledge in the pursuit of
education, learning, and research at the highest international levels of excellence.

www.cambridge.org
Information on this title: www.cambridge.org/9781108986915
DOI: 10.1017/9781108981828

© John P. Burgess 2022

This publication is in copyright. Subject to statutory exception
and to the provisions of relevant collective licensing agreements,
no reproduction of any part may take place without the written
permission of Cambridge University Press.

First published 2022

A catalogue record for this publication is available from the British Library.

ISBN 978-1-108-98691-5 Paperback
ISSN 2516-418X (online)
ISSN 2516-4171 (print)

Cambridge University Press has no responsibility for the persistence or accuracy of
URLs for external or third-party internet websites referred to in this publication
and does not guarantee that any content on such websites is, or will remain,
accurate or appropriate.

Set Theory

Elements in Philosophy and Logic

DOI: 10.1017/9781108981828
First published online: January 2022

John P. Burgess
Princeton University

Author for correspondence: John P. Burgess, jburgess@princeton.edu

Abstract: Set theory is a branch of mathematics with a special subject matter, the infinite, but also a general framework for all modern mathematics, whose notions figure in every branch, pure and applied. This Element will offer a concise introduction, treating the origins of the subject, the basic notion of set, the axioms of set theory and immediate consequences, the set-theoretic reconstruction of mathematics, and the theory of the infinite, touching also on selected topics from higher set theory, controversial axioms and undecided questions, and philosophical issues raised by technical developments.

Keywords: sets, infinity, continuum, cardinals, ordinals

© John P. Burgess 2022

ISBNs: 9781108986915 (PB), 9781108981828 (OC)
ISSNs: 2516-418X (online), 2516-4171 (print)

Contents

1 Historical Roots

Although in retrospect others (Bernard Bolzano, Richard Dedekind) can be viewed as precursors, set theory was largely the creation of a single individual, Georg Cantor, beginning in the 1870s, and his key work (Cantor, 1915) remains highly readable to this day. He launched the field with two results on questions with ancient roots.

1.1 Strings to Ordinals

Pythagoreans noted that if the lengths of otherwise similar strings are in the ratio 2:1, the shorter sounds an octave higher. Why? Because it vibrates twice as quickly. In modern mathematical language, if the graph of the displacement of the center of the string with time approximates $y = \cos x$ for the longer, it will approximate $y = \cos 2x$ for the shorter. No real string vibrates so simply, and a better approximation for the long string would be $y = a_1 \cos + a_2 \cos 2x$, with the amplitude a_1 of the "fundamental" much larger than the amplitude a_2 of the "overtone." By the eighteenth century, workers in analysis, the branch of mathematics beginning with calculus, were dealing with infinite trigonometric series:

$$y = (a_1 \cos x + b_1 \sin x) + (a_2 \cos 2x + b_2 \sin 2x) + (a_3 \cos 3x + b_3 \sin 3x) + \ldots$$

The "vibrating string controversy" engaging Leonhard Euler and others concerned how wide a class of functions can be represented in this form. The dispute exposed, beyond endemic deficiencies of rigor in the treatment of infinite series, lack of a common understanding about what is meant by a *function*. The ensuing nineteenth-century rigorization of analysis, besides banning any literal infinities or infinitesimals, explaining contexts containing the symbol ∞ without assuming it to denote anything in isolation, fixed on the maximally general notion of function, under which *any* correlation between inputs and outputs counts, as long as there is one and only one output per input. Improved rigor eventually led to consensus about the existence of trigonometric series representations.

But with existence there come uniqueness questions. Could a function have *two different* representations? Does the constant function zero have any other than the trivial one with $a_n = b_n = 0$ for all n? Bernhard Riemann showed it does not if the sequence converges for all x. But what if one allows an exceptional point for which convergence is not assumed? Enter Cantor. It turns out that even then triviality holds (and, as a conclusion, we get what we did not assume as a premise, convergence even at the exceptional point). Indeed, one can allow two or any finite number of exceptional points. One can even allow infinitely many as long as they are all *isolated* from one another, meaning that for each exceptional x there is a positive ε with no *other* exceptional points between $x - \varepsilon$ and $x + \varepsilon$. One can even allow a *doubly* exceptional point, not isolated from other exceptional points. Indeed, one can allow two or any finite number. One can even allow infinitely many as long as they are isolated from one another. One can even allow a *triply* exceptional point. And so on. And as one goes on, it becomes natural to switch from speaking in the plural of the exceptional points to speaking in the singular of the *set E* of which they are *elements*. What it means to treat E as a single item is to think of operations being applicable to it. The relevant operation on sets Cantor called *derivation*, discarding isolated points. Let E_0 be E itself, and let E_{n+1} be the derived set of E_n. Reimann's result was that uniqueness holds if $E_0 = \emptyset$, the empty set, with no elements. Cantor's results were that uniqueness holds if any of E_1, E_2, E_3, ... is empty. Moreover, if we let E_ω be the intersection of the E_n, the set of x belonging to all of them, uniqueness still holds if $E_\omega = \emptyset$. Moreover, the results continue, with sets indexed by:

$$\omega + 1, \omega + 2, \omega + 3, \ldots \omega + \omega = \omega \cdot 2, \omega \cdot 3, \omega \cdot 4, \ldots \omega \cdot \omega = \omega^2, \omega^3, \omega^4, \ldots \omega^\omega$$

and more. Here are Cantor's *transfinite ordinal numbers*, and, as the notation suggests, he introduced an arithmetic for them, with addition, multiplication, and exponentiation.

1.2 Quadrature to Cardinals

Euclid shows many geometrical figures can be constructed with straightedge and compass, indicating the steps involved and proving they lead to the desired result. Thus one can *duplicate the square*, or construct, given the side of a square, the side of a square of twice the area, just by taking the diagonal of the original square. To show a construction *not* possible is more difficult, and requires an analysis available only with the modern coordinate methods, which transform geometric into algebraic problems. Thus *duplicating the cube*, constructing, given the side of a cube, the side of a cube of twice the volume, turns out equivalent to obtaining a key number, $\sqrt[3]{2}$, from rational numbers by addition, subtraction, multiplication, division, and extraction of square roots. And this was proved impossible in the 1830s, disposing of an ancient problem. For *quadrature of the circle*, constructing for a given circle a square of equal area, the key number is π. Now, although $\sqrt[3]{2}$ is not obtainable in the way indicated, it is at least an *algebraic* number in the sense of a solution to a polynomial equation:

$$a_n x^n + a_{n-1} x^{n-1} + \ldots + a_1 x + a_0 = 0$$

with rational coefficients a_i, namely, $x^3-2 = 0$. It was conjectured, however, that π is not even algebraic in this sense. Joseph Liouville showed nonalgebraic or *transcendental* numbers exist. Then e, the basis of the natural logarithms, was shown to be one by Charles Hermite, and, finally, π by Ferdinand von Lindemann. Between these last two, Cantor showed that the vast majority of real numbers are transcendental.

Since the sets of algebraics and transcendentals are infinite, to say one has more elements than the other requires a definition of when the *transfinite cardinal*, or number of elements of one infinite set, A, is equal or unequal to that of another, B. Cantor took as his standard of equality the existence of a *bijection* between A and B, a relation under which each element of A is associated with exactly one element of B, and vice versa. In the case of the set N of natural numbers, the existence of a bijection with a set B means that the elements of B can be *enumerated* or listed in a sequence indexed by 0, 1, 2, ..., as in Table 1. An infinite set whose elements can be so enumerated is called *denumerable*, while a set that is *either* denumerable *or* finite is called *countable*.

The number of elements of a denumerable set Cantor called $\aleph_0$ (pronounced "aleph nought"). What the table shows is that signed integers and positive rationals both have cardinal or size $\aleph_0$; so do the signed rationals. Nowadays, a finite sequence of keystrokes is transmitted electronically as a sequence of zeros and ones, the binary numeral for some natural number that may be considered a code for the sequence. This makes the set of such sequences denumerable, in order of increasing code number. Then, since a polynomial equation of degree n has at most n solutions, each algebraic number can be denoted by an expression such as "the second smallest solution to $2x^3 - 9x^2 - 6x + 3 = 0$" and given a code number accordingly. But their denumerability was established in correspondence between Dedekind and Cantor long before the digital age began.

By contrast, Cantor showed that the whole set R of real numbers (and hence the set of transcendentals, left over when we remove the algebraics) is *not* denumerable. No countable set can contain even just those whose decimal

Table 1 Denumerable sets

Set	Enumeration									
Natural numbers	0	1	2	3	4	5	6	7	8	...
Integers	0	1	−1	2	−2	3	−3	4	−4	...
Positive rationals	1/1	1/2	2/1	1/3	2/3	3/2	3/1	1/4	3/4	...

Table 2 The diagonal argument

Index	Zero-one sequence								
0	0*	0	0	0	0	0	0	0	0	...
1	1	1*	1	1	1	1	1	1	1	...
2	0	1	0*	1	0	1	0	1	0	...
3	1	0	1	0*	1	0	1	0	1	...
...	...	...	...	...	...	...	...	...	...	...

expansion involves only 0s and 1s; or what is the same, all infinite zero-one sequences; or what is the same, all sets of natural numbers, each such being representable by the zero-one sequence with one in the nth place if and only if n is in the set. This he established by his famous *diagonal argument*. Suppose we have an enumeration of some set S of infinite zero-one sequences, as in Table 2. Go down the diagonal, marked with asterisks. Take in order for each n the digit appearing in the nth place in the nth row of the table. This gives 0100 .... Now swap the zeros and the ones. This gives 1011 ..., a sequence that does not belong to the denumerable set S, since it differs in the nth place from the nth sequence. Cantor called the cardinal of the real numbers or points of the line c. Analogously to the results in Table 1 in this discussion, he showed that the positive real numbers, or even just those in a finite interval, also have cardinal c, as do pairs of real numbers, or equivalently complex numbers. He also introduced an arithmetic, with addition, multiplication, and exponentiation, for his cardinals.

Cantor's audacious introduction of ω and $\aleph$ when mathematicians had just finished explaining away ∞ provoked a reaction. But Cantor's theory won acceptance among leaders in the rising generation fairly quickly (as examples they put forth, such as the one-, two-, and three-dimensional *Cantor set*, *Sierpinski carpet*, and *Menger sponge*, whose images appear all over the Internet today, captured the imagination of amateurs). The leading mathematician David Hilbert insisted: "No one shall expel us from the paradise Cantor created for us."

2 The Notion of Set

Many objections turned on certain *paradoxes*. Cantor, unlike his contemporary Gottlob Frege, never made the assumptions that led to these paradoxes, but he did not make clear enough what assumptions he *was* making. His successors had to be more clear and explicit. Explicit axiomatization began in the first decade of the twentieth century with Ernst Zermelo (1908/1967). His system, with additions and amendments, mainly by Abraham Fraenkel (1922/1967), remains that accepted today, when it is recognized that the paradoxes result mostly from confusing the notion of set behind the axioms of *Zermelo–Fraenkel set theory with Choice* (ZFC) with other ideas.

2.1 Collections

The expression "a multiplicity of objects" begins singular but ends plural, and may be understood as referring either to a *plurality*, a many, or to a *universal*, a one as opposed to a many. Universals include *properties*, which are *intensional*, meaning that two may be different even while having exactly the same instances, as with the stock example *being a coin in my pocket* and *being a penny in my pocket*, which are distinct properties even if I have no coins in my pocket but pennies. They also include *aggregates* completely determined by their components. One kind, topic of a theory called *mereology*, is a *fusion* of a plurality of component parts into a single whole, in a way that permits different pluralities to have the same fusion, as do the eight ranks and the eight files of a chessboard, the fusion being the selfsame chessboard in either case. By contrast we have *collections*, in which many are gathered into a one without losing track of which many they were.

The notion of collection in Frege (1893) was that of an *extension*. Here we start with all objects, and take what he called a *concept* (associated with a predicate), and divide objects into those that fall under the concept (satisfy the predicate) and those that do not. The collection of those that do is the extension of the concept, so that the extensions of two concepts are the same if and only if the concepts are *coextensive*, having exactly the same things falling under them. Graphically, we may represent the unbounded range of all objects with which we start as an unbounded blank page, and represent the extension as given by a dividing line or curve separating objects inside from objects outside, as in Figure 1. But for Frege, the extension is itself an object: If represented by a dot, that dot must fall on the page on one side or the other of the division – but which? That is the question indicated by the question marks in the figure.

Bertrand Russell raised an embarrassing issue about the extension R of the concept: it *is an extension that as an object is outside, not inside, itself*. In the case of the universal extension, V, the extension of *is self-identical*, V is inside itself since *everything* is inside V. In the case of the empty extension $\emptyset$, the extension of *nonself-identical*, $\emptyset$ is outside itself since *nothing* is inside $\emptyset$. Hence $\emptyset$ is inside, and V is outside, the Russell extension R. But just as the statement *this very statement is false* seems to be true if it is false and false if it is

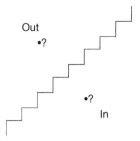

Figure 1 An extension

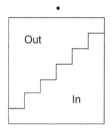

Figure 2 An ensemble

true, so R seems to be inside itself if outside itself, and outside if inside. This is the *Russell paradox* as Russell (1902) put it to Frege.

Contrasting with this inconsistent "top down" notion of extension is the "bottom up" notion of an *ensemble*. Here we start with a given "universe of discourse," which might be represented by a box, and a predicate will, like a curve in a Venn diagram, mark off the ensemble of things in the universe that do satisfy it from things in the universe that do not. The ensemble does *not*, however, itself belong to the universe. A dot representing it would lie outside the box, as in Figure 2. Implicit here is the possibility of *iteration*. We can add a new box atop the original, to accommodate all the dots representing ensembles of things in the lower box, and then more. But there are two ways to implement this idea.

On the *layered* approach of the *theory of types*, deriving from Russell (1908) by way of Frank Ramsey (1925), we have a hierarchy with *individuals* at the bottom type zero, collections called *classes* of type zero items at type one, classes of type one items at type two, and so on. Even if we assume *no* items at type zero, there will be one item at type one, the empty class $\emptyset_1$ of type zero items, and then two items at type two, the empty class $\emptyset_2$ of type one items, and the singleton class $\{\emptyset_1\}_2$ of the one item at type one. At type three, there will be four items, as in Table 3. With one item at type zero, there will be two at type

Table 3 The layered hierarchy

...	
4	Sixteen Items
3	$\varnothing_3$, $\{\varnothing_2\}_3$, $\{\{\varnothing_1\}_2\}_3$, $\{\varnothing_2,\{\varnothing_1\}_2\}_3$
2	$\varnothing_2$, $\{\varnothing_1\}_2$
1	$\varnothing_1$
0	No Items

one, then four, then sixteen. But with only finitely many individuals, there will only ever be only finitely many items of any one type. For mathematical purposes, Russell assumed infinitely many individuals.

2.2 Sets

By contrast, we have the *cumulative* approach, where successive boxes are nested, like Chinese boxes or Russian dolls, each higher one adding a new level of collections called *sets*. In box zero are individuals or *Urelemente*; at level one, sets whose elements are individuals; in box one, individuals and level-one sets; at level two, any new sets whose elements come from box one; in box two, box-one and level-two items; and so on.

In ZFC, we consider only *pure* sets, without individuals. There then will be no items at level zero, one item, the empty set $\varnothing$, at level one, in box one. As for level two, from the one item in box one can be formed two sets: the empty set $\varnothing$ and its singleton $\{\varnothing\}$, but the former we already have, so only the latter is new. In box three will be four items, two new at level three. In box four will be sixteen items, twelve new at level four. And so on, as in Table 4.

After all finite levels, we may recognize a box ω containing everything of finite level but nothing new, and then form a level $\omega + 1$ for sets whose elements come from level ω, meaning from any finite level, but do not themselves appear at any such level, containing as they do sets of arbitrarily high finite level. We can then continue through the transfinite ordinals. Zermelo at first claimed for his axioms only that they permitted none of the known deductions of contradictions, and seemed adequate to develop Cantor's set theory (as they are with Fraenkel's friendly amendments). Only later (as in Zermelo, 1930) did something like the picture in the table emerge.

The ideal of rigor is that one should list in advance all *primitives*, notions assumed meaningful without definition, and *postulates* or axioms, results assumed true without demonstration, and given these principles all further

Table 4 The cumulative hierarchy

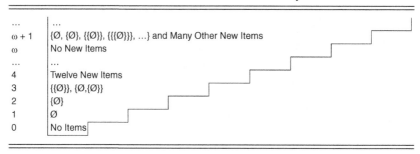

...	...
$\omega + 1$	{∅, {∅}, {{∅}}, {{{∅}}}, ...} and Many Other New Items
ω	No New Items
...	...
4	Twelve New Items
3	{{∅}}, {∅,{∅}}
2	{∅}
1	∅
0	No Items

Table 5 Primitive logical notions

Symbol	Operation	Reading
¬	Negation	"not"
∧	Conjunction	"and"
∨	Disjunction	"or"
∀	Universal quantification	"for all"
∃	Existential quantification	"for some" or "there exists"

notions or results should be logically derived, by definition or deduction. In set theory, there is just one primitive, written with a stylized epsilon symbol, $x \in y$, read "x is an element of y" or "x is in y" or "y contains x." All other notions must be defined in terms of this and the logical notion of identity using the logical operators in Table 5. A *formula* Φ is built up from *atomic* formulas $x \in y$ and $x = y$ using the five operations in the table.

Some minimal familiarity with logical notions and notations must be assumed here (for a quick review, see Boolos, Burgess, and Jeffrey, 2002, chapters 9 and 10), including an ability to recognize simple logical laws. In particular, familiarity is assumed with the distinction between "free" and "bound" occurrences of variables in a formula, those that are not and those that are caught by a quantifier. For example, in the formula asserting the non-emptiness of x, namely $\exists y(y \in x)$, the x is free but the y is bound. The latter could be changed to z without changing the meaning. Other logical and set-theoretic notions may be defined in terms of what we have so far, as in Tables 6 and 7, but officially these are mere abbreviations.

Table 6 Defined logical notions

Abbreviation	Definition	Operation	Reading
$\Phi \supset \Psi$	$\neg\Phi \vee \Psi$	Conditional	"if Φ then Ψ"
$\Phi \equiv \Psi$	$(\Phi \supset \Psi) \wedge (\Psi \supset \Phi)$	Biconditional	"Φ if and only if Ψ" or " Φ iff Ψ"
$x \neq y$	$\neg x = y$	Nonidentity	"x is distinct from y"
$\exists! x \Phi(x)$	$\exists x \forall y(\Phi(y) \equiv x = y)$	Unique existence	"there exists a unique"

Table 7 Defined set-theoretic notions

Abbreviation	Definition	Reading
$x \notin y$	$\neg\, x \in y$	"x is not an element of [or not in] y"
$x \subseteq y$	$\forall z\, (z \in x \supset z \in y)$	"x is a subset of [or included in] y"
$\forall x \in y\, \Phi(x)$	$\forall x(x \in y \supset \Phi(x))$	"for all x in y ..."
$\exists x \in y\, \Phi(x)$	$\exists x(x \in y \wedge \Phi(x))$	"for some x in y ..."

3 The Zermelo–Fraenkel Axioms

The axioms of the system ZFC will be presented next, in both words and symbols, to be assumed without proof, but not without something in the way of informal, intuitive justification.

3.1 Statement

The first axiom says sets with the same elements are the same. It has two equivalent formulations:

Extensionality (1) $\forall z(z \in x \equiv z \in y) \supset x = y$, **(2)** $x \subseteq y \wedge y \subseteq x \supset x = y$.

By convention, in displaying formulas initial universal quantifiers are omitted, so what is meant is really $\forall x \forall y(\_\_)$ where what is explicitly written is $\_\_$. As (2) suggests, proofs of identities most often come in two parts, proving inclusion in two directions. Extensionality implies that if there is a set y whose elements are all and only the sets x satisfying a condition Φ, it is unique. That unique set, if it exists, is denoted $\{x|\,\Phi(x)\}$, and we have $z \in \{x|\,\Phi(x)\}$ if $\Phi(z)$. Frege's inconsistent assumption would be an axiom of *comprehension*, according to which

$\{x| \Phi(x)\}$ *always* exists for *any* condition Φ. Applied to the condition $x \notin x$ this would give the Russell paradox, and it is not assumed in ZFC.

The second axiom says that if we *already have* some set u, we can at least separate out from u those of its elements that satisfy a condition Φ to form $\{x \in u | \Phi(x)\}$:

Separation $\exists y \forall x (x \in y \equiv (x \in u \wedge \Phi(x)))$.

This is not a single formula, but rather a rule to the effect that anything of a certain *form* counts as an axiom. The cases for different Φ are called *instances* of the *scheme* of separation. (Zermelo's original formulation was vaguer.) Note that separation implies there is no *universal set* of all sets $V = \{x | x = x\}$. If there were, we could, by separation, obtain comprehension.

Further axioms state the existence of certain specific sets:

Pairing $\exists y \, (u \in y \wedge v \in y)$.
Union $\exists y \, \forall z \in X \, \forall x \in z (x \in y)$.

With what we have so far, some basic existence results then become deducible, those in Table 8. (The expression "family" used in the table may be used for any set of sets.)

Separation gives us the empty set, since given any set u at all – and even pure logic assumes there is at least one item in the domain our quantifiers range over, which in the present case consists of sets – separation gives $\{x \in u | x \notin u\}$, which is empty. It also gives twofold intersections, and by the alternative definition, family intersections, if the family X has at least one member u; also differences. Now given y containing u and v, we can separate out the elements of y identical to one of those two, so pairing with separation gives the unordered pair. Union with separation gives us family union. The unordered triple and twofold union we then get using the alternative definitions. The difference $u - v$ is also called the *relative* complement of v in u. An *absolute* complement $-v = \{x | x \notin v\}$ cannot exist, because $v \cup -v$ would be the nonexistent V.

The next two axioms are these:

Power $\exists y \forall x (x \subseteq u \supset x \in y)$.
Infinity $\exists y (\emptyset \in y \wedge \forall x \in y (\{x\} \in y))$.

Power with separation gives the *power set* $\mathcal{P}(x) = \{y | y \subseteq x\}$ and also

$\{y \subseteq x | \Phi(y)\} = \{y \in \mathcal{P}(x) | \Phi(y)\}$.

Table 8 More defined notions

Name	Symbol	Definition	Alternatively
Empty set	$\emptyset$	$\{x \mid x \neq x\}$	
Singleton	$\{u\}$	$\{x \mid x = u\}$	$\{u,\, u\}$
Unordered pair	$\{u, v\}$	$\{x \mid x = u \lor x = v\}$	
Unordered triple	$\{u, v, w\}$	$\{x \mid x = u \lor x = v \lor x = w\}$	$\{u, v\} \cup \{w\}$
Twofold untersection	$u \cap v$	$\{x \mid x = u \land x = v\}$	$\{x \in u \mid x \in v\}$
Family intersection	$\cap X$	$\{x \mid \forall z(z \in X \supset x \in z)\}$	$\{x \in u \mid \forall z(z \in X \supset x \in z)\}$
Twofold union	$u \cup v$	$\{x \mid x = u \lor x = v\}$	$\cup \{u, v\}$
Family union	$\cup X$	$\{x \mid \exists z(z \in X \land x \in z)\}$	
Difference	$u - v$	$\{x \mid x \in u \land x \notin v\}$	$\{x \in u \mid x \notin v\}$

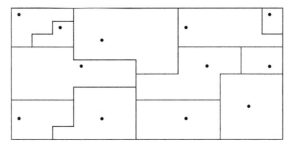

Figure 3 Partition and selector

Infinity guarantees the existence of a set that contains all of $\emptyset$ and $\{\emptyset\}$ and $\{\{\emptyset\}\}$ and so on, and hence is infinite; alternative formulations are possible; more detailed discussion is postponed.

Also postponed is detailed discussion, beyond its mere statement, of the widely known axiom of choice (AC), pictured in Figure 3.

Sets whose intersection is nonempty are said to *meet* or *overlap*; those whose intersection is empty are called *disjoint*, and a family any two members of which are disjoint is called *pairwise disjoint*, a family of nonempty, pairwise disjoint sets is called a *partition* (of its union), and the members of the family the *cells* thereof. Axiom of choice asserts that for any *partition* there is a *selector*, a set containing exactly one element from each cell (represented in the figure by the scattered dots). Alone of the axioms, AC asserts the existence of a set satisfying a certain condition, without given a definition of such a set as $\{x|\Phi(x)\}$ for any Φ:

Choice $\forall X(\forall x \in X(x \neq \emptyset) \wedge \forall x \in X \forall y \in X(x \neq y \supset x \cap y = \emptyset)$
$\supset \exists Y \forall x \in X \exists! y \in Y(y \in x)).$

Fraenkel's distinctive addition to Zermelo's axioms, replacement, is a scheme saying that if to each element x of a set u there is associated a unique y satisfying a condition $\Phi(x, y)$ – call it $\varphi(x)$ – we may replace each x in u by $\varphi(x)$ and form the set $\{\varphi(x)|x \in u\}$. Actually, it is enough to assume there is a set containing all $\varphi(x)$ for $x \in u$ and then apply separation to get the set of all *and only* the $\varphi(x)$ for $x \in u$. So, the new assumption we need is this:

Replacement $\forall x \in u \exists! y \Phi(x, y) \supset \exists v \forall x \in u \exists y \in v \Phi(x, y).$

3.2 Motivation

While "intuition" may not be appealed to in proofs of theorems, still where axioms are connected with an intuitive picture, it may at least suggest conjectures, besides being a source of confidence in the consistency of an axiom system, beyond the mere inductive consideration that no contradiction has been found so far. For such reasons, interest attaches to the relationship between the axioms of ZFC (beyond extensionality) and the cumulative hierarchy picture.

For separation, the nonexistence of a universal set V is clear, since the elements of a set that at a given level come from lower levels. By contrast, if a set x appears at a given level, then its elements all appear at lower levels, including such of them as satisfy some condition Φ, and hence the set of all such will appear at a level no higher than that of x itself.

For pairing, if u appears at some level and v at some level, one of these levels will have to be no earlier than the other, and both u and v will be present at that level, and so $\{u, v\}$ should appear at the very next. For union, if X appears at some level, every element appears at some earlier level and every element of such an element at some still earlier, so all elements of elements will be present at levels below that of X, and the set $\cup X$ present by the same level as X. For power, if u appears at some level, then we have seen all its subsets are present by that level, and so $\mathcal{P}(u)$ should appear at the very next. For infinity, it asserts no more than the existence of such a set as we see at level $\omega + 1$ in Table 4 in Section 2.2.

For choice, if a partition X occurs at some level, it is easily seen any selector for it will appear by that same level. But *is* there any selector? The assumption that the hierarchy is maximally "wide," admitting at a given level *all* sets that could conceivably be formed from elements at lower levels, means that we should not be imposing any requirement of *definability* as a precondition for set existence. Historically, objections to AC have generally rested on implicit imposition of some such precondition, so the cumulative hierarchy picture excludes the major *anti*choice argument. But that is not quite to say that it provides a substantive *pro*choice argument, and the axiom remains, to a degree, controversial. Although it is no longer common for working mathematicians to star theorems whose proof depends on AC, set theorists keep track.

For replacement, many feel the understanding that the cumulative hierarchy is supposed to be maximally "high," admitting *all* levels that could conceivably be admitted, supports the axiom. But here the influence may be felt of what some would claim is a *further* thought, a doctrine of *limitation of size*, according to which all that can prevent a plurality of sets from being collected together into a set would be there being *too many* of them. (Cantor distinguished the *inconsistent* multiplicities that cannot be collected into a whole from the *consistent* ones that can by the formers' being *absolutely infinite* where the latter are only *transfinite*.) The idea would be that in $\{\varphi(x)|x \in u\}$ there would not be too many elements to form a set, since there would be no more than there are in u, which already *is* a set. See Boolos (1971) for critical discussion.

There remains an axiom not always counted as part of ZFC – and, in particular, not so counted in at least one widely used introductory textbook – although so counted here. It has two equivalent formulations.

Foundation $(1)\, \forall x (x \neq \emptyset \supset \exists y\, x\, \forall z\, x\, (z \notin y))$,
$(2)\, \forall x (x \neq \emptyset \supset \exists y \in x\, (y \cap x = \emptyset))$.

In words, if x has any elements at all, then it has an element y that is *epsilon minimal*, meaning that there is no other element z with $z \in y$. The axiom, which also goes by the alias *regularity*, is directly suggested by the cumulative hierarchy picture: If x has any elements, it must have an element y of lowest possible level for an element of x, and such a y will be epsilon minimal. Some immediate consequences:

There is no set x with $x \in x$.
There are no sets x, y with $x \in y \in x$.
There are no sets x, y, z with $x \in y \in z \in x$.

Why not? Because $\{x\}$ or $\{x,\ y\}$ or $\{x,\ y,\ z\}$, as the case may be, would have no epsilon-minimal element. The axiom also excludes the existence of any infinite descending chain with $x_1 \in x_0$ and $x_2 \in x_1$ and $x_3 \in x_2$ and so on. Alongside orthodox set theory ZFC, there exist heterodox "alternative" set theories. Incurvati (2020) surveys several, including two that permit infinite descending sequences: a "graph" conception due to Peter Aczel and a "stratified" conception due to W. V. Quine. (He also considers a "paraconsistent" conception that accepts comprehension and the Russell paradox, but adopts a deviant logic in hopes of quarantining the contradiction.) See also Holmes (2017).

4 Immediate Consequences

Some consequences of the axioms were established well before set theory became a separate subject.

4.1 The Algebra of Sets

An important step toward modern logic was taken by George Boole, whose *Laws of Thought* (1854) contains formulas in algebraic symbolism each admitting two readings: as a principle of logic and as what we recognize retrospectively as a one of set theory. Thus the formula $a \cdot b = b \cdot a$ expresses both the logical law of the commutativity of conjunction, $\Phi \wedge \Psi$ iff $\Psi \wedge \Phi$, and the set-theoretic law of the commutativity of intersection, $x \cap y = y \cap x$. Suppose we are working for a time only with subsets of some given set I, and allow ourselves to write $-x$ for $I - x$. Then the first batch of theorems of ZFC consists of equations of so-called *Boolean algebra* for $\cap$ and $\cup$ and $-$. The proof of such an equation consists in applying extensionality after showing that any item will belong to the right side if it belongs to the left side; and the proof of *that* consists in unpacking the definitions and applying a law of logic, the very law that in Boole's notation would be expressed by the same algebraical formula as the set-theoretic result we are trying to prove, thus:

$$z \in x \cap y \ \text{iff} \ z \in x \wedge z \in y \ \text{iff} \ z \in y \wedge z \in x \ \text{iff} \ z \in y \cap x.$$

Any number of further laws of the algebra of sets are found in Table 9, in pairs of "dual" laws on the same row. Another, not in the table, is the law $- - x = x$, corresponding to the law of *double negation*: $\neg\neg \ \Phi$ iff Φ.

Further laws involving inclusion appear in Table 10. Many of these laws may be familiar from school, where they might have been illustrated by Venn diagrams. Even an introductory textbook of set theory, although it might run to hundreds of pages, would leave the verification of most as "exercises for the reader" – with the good excuse that, in any case, one can only really learn a mathematical subject by doing exercises – and in this much shorter Element, where the aim must be less to train the reader *in* than to inform the reader *about* a technical subject, they will *all* be so left. (The proofs do not *all* have to be proceed "elementwise," as in the commutative law example. Once one has accumulated a few laws, others can be derived from them "algebraically," without going back to the definitions.)

4.2 The Algebra of Relations

Boole's logic covers a bit more than Aristotelian syllogistic, being a version of the modern logic of *one-place* predicates. It is still not enough to analyze serious mathematical arguments, which generally involve *two-place* predicates (such as $\in$). The logic of many-place predicates in present-day textbooks derives from Frege (1879) conceptually, and Giuseppe Peano and others notationally, but even before them, there were attempts to develop predicate logic in Boole's algebraic style.

To incorporate relation theory into set theory we must identify relations with sets of some kind. The first step is to ignore the distinction between a relation R such as *parent of* and what is sometimes called the "graph" of the relation, the set of ordered pairs (a, b) with a a parent of b. We write Rab or aRb or $(a, b) \in R$ indifferently. The second step is to identify an ordered pair (a, b) with a set of some kind, most commonly using the *Wiener–Kuratowski* definition:

Table 9 Boolean laws

Name	Symbolic statement	
Commutative	$x \cap y = y \cap x$	$x \cup y = y \cup x$
Associative	$x \cap (y \cap z) = (x \cap y) \cap z$	$x \cup (y \cup z) = (x \cup y) \cup z$
Distributive	$x \cap (y \cup z) = (x \cap y) \cup (x \cap z)$	$x \cap (y \cup z) = (x \cup y) \cap (x \cup z)$
Idempotent	$x \cap x = x$	$x \cup x = x$
Identity	$-I = \emptyset$	$-\emptyset = I$
	$x \cap I = x$	$x \cup \emptyset = x$
	$x \cap \emptyset = \emptyset$	$x \cup I = I$
Complement	$x \cap -x = \emptyset$	$x \cup -x = I$
De Morgan	$-(x \cap y) = -x \cup -y$	$-(x \cup y) = -x \cap -y$

Table 10 More Boolean laws

Name	Symbolic statement	
Reflexivity	$x \subseteq x$	
Antisymmetry	if $x \subseteq y \wedge y \subseteq x \supset x = y$	
Transitivity	if $x \subseteq y \wedge y \subseteq z \supset x \subseteq z$	
Extrema	$\emptyset \subseteq x \wedge x \subseteq y$	
Complementarity	$x \subseteq y \equiv -y \subseteq -x$	
Lattice laws	$x \subseteq y \equiv x \cap y = x$	$x \subseteq y \equiv x \cup y = y$
	$x \subseteq y \wedge x \subseteq z \supset x \subseteq y \cap z$	$x \subseteq z \wedge y \subseteq z \supset x \cup y \subseteq z$

$$(a, b) = \{\{a\}, \{a, b\}\}.$$

It would be idle to pretend this reveals what ordered pairs have been all along. It is an attempt to define something with all the features of ordered pairs *needed for mathematics*, without going beyond set theory. Its acceptability depends on prior analysis of just what *is* needed for mathematics. The consensus is that the existence for every a and b of a unique ordered pair (a, b), together with the following fundamental law of pairs, will do:

Fundamental Law of Pairs $(a, b) = (c, d)$ iff $a = b \wedge c = d$.

Given the Wiener–Kuratowski definition, the existence of the ordered pair follows by three applications of pairing to get $\{a\}$ and $\{a, b\}$ and then (a, b). The proof of the fundamental law will be left as an exercise. One also needs, for any A and B, the existence of the Cartesian product:

$$A \otimes B = \{(a, b) | a \in A \wedge b \in B\} = \{x | \exists a \in A \exists b \in B(x = (a, b))\}.$$

There are two interestingly different proofs. The first begins by noting that we have already the existence of the union of A and B, of the power set of that union, and of the power set of the power set; while also each of $\{a\}$ and $\{a, b\}$ is a subset of the union and hence (a, b) defined the Wiener–Kuratowski way is a subset of its power set. Separation then gives what we want:

$$A \otimes B = \{x \subseteq \mathcal{P}(A \cup B) | \exists a \in A \exists b \in B(x = \{\{a\}, \{a, b\}\})\}.$$

The second begins by applying replacement twice to conclude:

Table 11 Defined relation-theoretic notions

Name	Symbol	Definition
Domain	dom R	$\{a \mid \exists b \; aRb\}$
Range	ran R	$\{b \mid \exists a \; aRb\}$
Restriction	$R \mid C$	$\{(x, \; b) \in R \mid x \in C\}$
Image	$R[C]$	$\{b \mid \exists x \in C \; xRb\}$
Inverse	R^{-1}	$\{(b, \; a) \mid aRb\}$
Composition	$R \circ S$	$\{(a, c) \mid \exists b \in B \; (aRb \wedge bRc)\}$

$\{a\} \otimes B = \{(a,b) \mid b \in B\}$ exists for each $a \in A$.

$\{\{a\} \otimes B \mid a \in A\}$ exists.

Then $A \otimes B = \cup \; \{\{a\} \otimes B \mid a \in A\}$ exists.

There is a host of definitions that can now be made, some assembled in Table 11. (It is traditional to illustrate some of them by kinship relations. Thus the inverse of *parent of* is *child of* and the composition of *sister of* and *parent of* is *aunt of*.) Note that in the table the a and the b in dom R and ran R will automatically belong to $\cup \cup R$ under the Wiener–Kuratowski definition, so domain and range exist by separation. We leave the existence question in the other cases to the reader. There are other terms in use: the inverse of R is alternatively called the *converse*, while $R^{-1}[D]$ is called the *preimage* of D, and dom $R \cup$ ran R the *field* of R.

Students of mathematics encounter these definitions gradually in the course of studying this or that branch of mathematics, rather than in a bloc in a separate course on set theory. Readers encountering the lot all at once may think of learning them as like learning vocabulary in a foreign language, and try to absorb a few each day.

These notions are connected by an endless list of little laws, such as $R[C] = $ ran $R \mid C$, that follow at once from the definitions. Such laws occupy page after weary page in the first volume of Whitehead and Russell's monumental *Principia Mathematica* (1910). A few are usually singled out for special mention:

$$(R \circ S)^{-1} = S^{-1} \circ R^{-1} \qquad (R \circ S) \circ T = R \circ (S \circ T).$$

$$R[C \cup D] = R[C] \cup R[D] \qquad R[C \cap D] \subseteq R[C] \cap R[D].$$

There is also special vocabulary for special features a relation may or may not possess, shown in Table 12 (wherein defining conditions are supposed to hold

Table 12 Properties of relations

Name	Definition
Reflexive	aRa
Irreflexive	$\neg aRa$
Symmetric	$aRb \supset bRa$
Antisymmetric	$aRb \wedge bRa \supset a = b$
Transitive	$aRb \wedge bRc \supset aRc$
Connected (reflexive case)	$aRb \vee bRa$
Connected (irreflexive case)	$aRb \vee a = b \vee bRa$

for *all a, b, c* in the field of the relation). Officially, a relation is a *set* of ordered pairs, so since there is no *set* of *all* pairs (x, y) such that $x \in y$ – the assumption that there is can without much difficulty be shown to imply the existence of a universal set – elementhood is not a relation in the official sense; neither is inclusion $\subseteq$. We can still call them relation*ships*, and apply the terminology in the table. (There is a variant NBG of ZFC in which they are treated more formally as "classes," collections assumed over and above sets.) Thus inclusion is reflexive, elementhood irreflexive.

4.3 Functions, Orders, Equivalences

For future reference, definitions will be collected now pertaining to three kinds of relation ubiquitous in mathematics. This material, admittedly a bit dry until we are ready to take up substantive examples, may be skimmed and referred back to as needed later. A *function* is a relation R such that for any a in dom R there is a *unique b* in ran R with aRb. Often one uses lowercase letters f, g for functions. The unique b with afb is called the *value* or output for *argument* or input a, and denoted $f(a)$. If, additionally, for any b in the range there is exactly one a in the domain with $f(a) = b$, the function f is called *injective*. The notation $f: A \to B$ indicates that f is a function with dom $f = A$ and ran $f \subseteq B$. If ran $f = B$, then the function is called *surjective* with respect to B, while *bijective* means both injective and surjective, and a function that is in- or sur- or bijective is called an *in-* or *sur-* or *bijection*. (Older terminology was "one-to-one" and "onto" and "correspondence.") In certain contexts, it proves convenient to write the values of a function X with dom $X = I$ not as $X(i)$ but as X_i. With this notation, we write the range as $\{X_i \mid i \in I\}$ and call it an *indexed family* with *index set I*. The DeMorgan and distributive laws of Table 9 in Section 4.2, among others, generalize to indexed families:

$$-\cap\{X_i|i\in I\} = \cup\{-X_i|i\in I\} \qquad -\cup\{X_i|i\in I\} = \cap\{-X_i|i\in I\}.$$

$$X\cap(\cup\{Y_i|i\in I\}) = \cup\{X\cap Y_i|i\in I\} \quad X\cup(\cap\{Y_i|i\in I\}) = \cap\{X\cup Y_i|i\in I\}.$$

A *two-place* function is simply a function whose arguments are ordered pairs, but we write $f(a,b)$ rather than $f((a,b))$ for simplicity. Note that, officially, a function is a *set* of ordered pairs, so we cannot call intersection and union two-place functions. We call them *operations*, and apply the same terminology of "associative" and "commutative" and so on to them as to two-place functions.

It is easily seen that *identity* on a set A, $i = \{(a,a)|a\in A\}$ is a function; also that the inverse f^{-1} of a function f is a function if f is an injection. Also, the composition $f\circ g$ for functions f and g is a function if ran $f\subseteq$ dom g. A good exercise is to verify that the identity function is a bijection, that the inverse of a bijection is a bijection, and that the composition of two bijections is a bijection. Then if we define two sets to be *equipollent* or *equinumerous* if there is a bijection between them, as Cantor did, it follows that equipollence or equinumerosity is a reflexive, symmetric, and transitive relationship.

Notice that under the definitions used so far, beginning from what is the most natural definition of composition when working on the general theory of relations, we get for functions that $(f\circ g)(a) = g(f(a))$, where in the notation the order of f and g get switched. The more usual approach in mainstream mathematics, which rather seldom considers composition of relations other than functions, modifies the definition so as to get the result $(g\circ f)(a) = g(f(a))$.

A *partial order* is a relation that is reflexive, antisymmetric, and transitive. Often we write $\leq$ or a similar symbol for a partial order, and then use related notations in more or less obvious senses:

$$x\leq y\leq z \text{ iff } x\leq y \text{ and } y\leq z \qquad x\geq y \text{ iff } y\leq x \qquad x<y \text{ iff } x\leq y \text{ but } x\neq y.$$

A *minimal* element x of a set X is one such that for no y in X is $y<x$. A *minimum* or *least* is one such that for all y in X we have $x\leq y$. The terms *maximal* and *maximum* or *greatest* are used analogously. The minimal *versus* minimum distinction collapses, allowing both to be abbreviated *min*, for connected partial orders, called *total* or *linear* orders or simply *orders*. A *chain* in a partial order is a subset C of its field connected by $\leq$. A *wellorder* is one in which every nonempty subset of the field has a least element. A set is *wellorderable* if there exists some wellorder on it (in which case, there will also exist others). Sometimes, it is more convenient to start with the notion of a *strict* order $<$, a relation that is irreflexive, transitive, and connected, and think of $\leq$ as defined in terms of $<$.

In modern mathematics, a *structure* A is a nonempty set $A \neq \emptyset$ equipped with extra apparatus, which in the only case of interest here will be simply a two-place relation $R \subseteq A \otimes A$. A function $f \colon A \to B$ is an *isomorphism* between structures $\mathbf{A} = (A, R)$ and $\mathbf{B} = (B, S)$ if it is a bijection and further *preserves* the relevant relation, meaning that if $f(a) = b$ and $f(c) = d$, then aRc iff bSd. In the case of sets with orders A, B, since the sets A, B are simply the fields of the relation R, S, for ordinary purposes one hardly distinguishes between the structures and their relations, speaking of structures as orders and of isomorphism between relations. $B = (B, S)$ is a *substructure* of $A = (A, R)$ iff $B \subseteq A$ and S is the restriction $R \cap (B \otimes B)$ of R to B. When the set A is a family of subsets of some set I, so $A \subseteq \mathcal{P}(I)$, we will write $X \in A$ when we really mean (A, R) where R is the restriction of inclusion to A, the set of pairs (X, Y) with $(A, \subseteq)$ and $Y \in A$ and $X \subseteq Y$. $(A, \in)$ is understood similarly. For example, $(\mathcal{P}(I), \subseteq)$ is a partial order with minimum $\emptyset$, and its substructure $(\mathcal{P}^*(I), \subseteq)$, where $\mathcal{P}^*(I) = \mathcal{P}(I) - \{\emptyset\}$, the family of non-empty subsets of I, is a partial order in which every singleton $\{a\}$ is minimal, but there is no minimum. If $f \colon I \to J$ is a bijection, then there is an "induced" isomorphism F between $(\mathcal{P}(I), \subseteq)$, and $(\mathcal{P}(J), \subseteq)$ given by $F(A) = f[A]$. A good exercise is to check that the identity function is an isomorphism, that the inverse of an isomorphism is an isomorphism, and that the composition of two isomorphisms is an isomorphism. Then if we call structures *isomorphic* when there exists an isomorphism between them, it will follow that "isomorphism" in the sense of "being isomorphic" is a reflexive, symmetric, and transitive relationship.

An *equivalence* relation is one that is reflexive, symmetric, and transitive. We often write E or some equals-sign-like symbol for an equivalence. The term is also applied to relationships, including equinumerosity $\approx$ and isomorphism $\cong$. Given a function f with domain A the relation aEb that holds if $f(a) = f(b)$ is an equivalence. So if X is a partition of I, then considering $f(a) =$ the unique cell $[a]$ of X to which a belongs, we see that *belonging to the same cell* is an equivalence on I. Inversely, if we start with an equivalence E on I and let $[a] = \{b : aEb\}$, the family X of all $[a]$ is a partition of I. (To see that the $[a]$ are nonempty and that $\cup X = I$, use the reflexivity of E to conclude $a \in [a]$. Symmetry and transitivity can be used to show that for all a and b, if aEb then $[a] = [b]$, while if $\neg aEb$ then $[a] \cap [b] = \emptyset$.) Equivalence and partition are twins. The cell $[a]$ is traditionally called the "equivalence class" of a. All the foregoing notions can be further exemplified once we have the traditional number systems available.

5 Number Systems Within Set Theory

A history of modern mathematics in about 300 words: It began building on a heritage summed up in two writers. Euclid's *Elements* presented the ideal of rigor and its partial realization in geometry. Al-Khwarizmi (whose name gives us our word *algorithm*) in his *al-Jabr w'al-Muqabala* (whose title gives us our word *algebra*) transmitted solutions of linear and quadratic equations. The first modern contributions began with the solution to cubic equations, where already we see a key modern feature, solving problems in one mathematical realm by bringing in another: Real roots of cubics are found by introducing "imaginaries." Then followed the development of an efficient algebraic notation, and the coordinate methods of analytic geometry, leading to algebraic solutions to geometric problems – at the cost of compromising the rigor of pure geometry. The analytic approach to ancient problems of tangency and quadrature led to the calculus and its notions of *derivative* and *integral*, which take us back and forth between a quantity varying with time and its rate of change, and provide apparatus for physics – at the cost of difficulties over infinities. The introduction of ever-new structures (non-Euclidean geometries, noncommutative algebras) continued apace in the nineteenth century, when rigor began to be firmed up. The interaction of different branches of mathematics meant a need for not just rigorous treatments of various branches separately, but a unified system, and one flexible enough to accommodate an endlessly growing array of novelties. The kind of framework needed was eventually provided by ZFC, and the reconstruction of mathematics on a set-theoretic basis became the theme of a French group writing a vast encyclopedia under the pseudonym Bourbaki, beginning with "his" (1939). The most important devices used can be seen at work already in the set-theoretic construction of the higher number systems (integral, rational, real, complex) out of the natural numbers, themselves explained set theoretically. This reconstruction is all that can be discussed here, and even it only in outline.

5.1 Real to Complex

Reconstruction of the traditional number systems proceeded in the reverse of the historical order of their introduction, in five steps, explaining a higher system in terms of a lower one taken for granted: (i) the complexes $\mathbf{C}$ in terms of the reals, (ii) the reals $\mathbf{R}$ in terms of the rationals, (iii) the rationals $\mathbf{Q}$ in terms of the integers, (iv) the integers $\mathbf{Z}$ in terms of the naturals, and (v) the naturals $\mathbf{N}$ in terms of set theory. Here (i), (ii), and (v) will be sketched, (iii) and (iv), being much like (i), and nowadays covered alongside it in textbooks of abstract algebra, as (ii) is in textbooks of analysis. For more detail, this material was first made available in one place to undergraduates in Landau (1930), which remains highly readable.

At no stage was a new rigorous definition of a number system put forward as an account of what the numbers in question had really been all along, faithful to the ideas – in fact, often hazy – of the first to study it. As regards step (v) this fact is emphasized in the philosophical classic Benacerraf (1965), but it holds generally. The search was for a surrogate system with all the properties traditionally assumed that are *important for mathematics*. Such a project presupposes consensus about what the mathematically important properties *are*. They are perhaps most easily identified in the case of the complex numbers. Each is a sum $a + bi$ of a real a and a real multiple b of the "imaginary" unit i, and they are added and multiplied according to the following rules:

$$(a + bi) + (c + di) = (a + c) + (b + d)i$$
$$(a + bi) \cdot (c + di) = (a \cdot c - b \cdot d) + (a \cdot d + b \cdot c)i.$$

That is all. In the case of the reals and naturals, the needed identification of mathematically important properties is due mainly to Dedekind: for the reals in *Stetigkeit und irrationale Zahlen*, for the naturals in *Was sind und was sollen die Zahlen?*, available together in English as Dedekind (1901).

In the complex or 'imaginary' case, around 1800 several workers independently came up with a geometric interpretation of complex numbers as points in the plane, still taught in schools. The great C. F. Gauss remarked that if instead of *positive*, *negative*, and *imaginary* one had spoken of *forwards*, *backwards*, and *sideways*, there would never have even seemed to be any mystery. In coordinate geometry, a plane point is represented by a pair of reals, and so one can simply identify $a + bi$ with (a, b) and stipulate the desired arithmetic rules:

$$(a, b) + (c, d) = (a + c, b + d) \quad (a, b) \cdot (c, d) = (a \cdot c - b \cdot d, a \cdot d + b \cdot c).$$

It is a tedious but routine exercise to derive the usual commutative, associative, and distributive laws for the complexes from these definitions and the same laws for the reals.

Generalization motivates rigorization: The introduction of unfamiliar structures, where the reliability becomes doubtful of intuitions developed from work with more familiar ones, was one reason for closer attention to rigor. Inversely, rigorization often opened up the prospect of innovations. If *pairs* can be added and multiplied, what about *triples* or *quadruples*, or whatever? W. R. Hamilton found that there is no reasonable multiplication rule for triples, but that there *is* one for quadruples, and thus he arrived at the *quaternions* expounded in

Hamilton (1853). Once a construction has given us the mathematically important properties, mathematicians might as well forget about it, *except that* they may want to come back to it when seeking to do something analogous elsewhere.

5.2 Rational to Real

Rigorous Greek mathematics recognized no zero and no negative numbers, and not even positive real numbers, but only ratios of geometric magnitudes such as line segments. Neither did it recognize even positive rational numbers, but only ratios of positive natural numbers, with ratios themselves scarcely considered independently of questions of *proportionality* or equality of ratios, the first is to the second as the third is to the fourth. Taking proportionality for natural numbers to be understood, proportionality for line segments can be made sense of whenever a ratio of segments $A:B$ can be equated with a ratio of natural numbers $m:n$. This can be done when dividing B into n equal pieces and laying off m of them along A, they exactly fill it. If they fall short or go beyond, $A:B$ is greater or less, as the case may be, than $m:n$. What is often anachronistically described as the Greek discovery that $\sqrt{2}$ is irrational was actually the discovery that the ratio of diagonal to side in a square is not the same as any ratio of natural numbers. How, then, can proportionality for segments in general be defined? The solution of Eudoxos, found in Euclid, Book V, in effect declares $A : B$ equal to $C : D$ if for every m and n, if either of the two segmentratios is greater than m: n, then so is the other. For us, for whom ratios of natural numbers are rational numbers and ratios of line segments are real numbers, this says that *a real number is completely determined by the set of rational numbers less than it.*

Early modern mathematics had an account of what (signed) real numbers are: ratios of lengths of (directed) line segments. Certain Euclidean straightedge and compass constructions can be interpreted as adding and multiplying ratios, making them *numbers* in the sense of things one can add and multiply. And the usual commutative, associative, and distributive laws can be deduced well-known geometric theorems. This is the standpoint explicit in Isaac Newton's *Universal Arithmetic* and implicit in René Descartes' *Geometry*, and it seems to go back to at least Omar Khayyam. By the nineteenth century, especially after the advent of non-Euclidean geometries, it came to seem desirable to provide a new, nongeometric, purely arithmetical-algebraic understanding. This is what is done by Dedekind (and independently in a different way by Cantor). Dedekind removed the geometric scaffolding and, in effect, simply identified a real number with the set of rational numbers less than it. Needless to say, as a definition, "a real number is the set of rational numbers less than some real number" is hopelessly circular. The trick must be to characterize the relevant sets of rational numbers *without* presupposing reals. The Dedekind identification is with a *cut* in the rationals, a set A with three features: (i) A is neither $\varnothing$ nor the whole of $\mathbf{Q}$; (ii) every element of A is less than every nonelement; (iii) A has no largest element. If these are taken as the real numbers, we can define the order relation $\leq$ on them simply as the inclusion relation $\subseteq$. It is necessary to define also the arithmetic operations and show that the usual laws apply, which Dedekind did, giving as he claimed the first rigorous proof that $\sqrt{2} \cdot \sqrt{3} \cdot \sqrt{6}$.

For Dedekind, the crucial property of the real numbers going beyond the basic laws of algebra that hold already for the rationals, was *continuity*, equivalent to what is known as the *least upper bound* (LUB) *principle*. Here an upper bound for a set A is a y with $x \leq y$ for every x in A. and a *least* upper bound (LUB) is an upper bound y such that $y \leq z$ for any other upper bound z. The LUB principle says that any nonempty set with an upper bound has a *least* one, and this is indeed just what is needed for the "intermediate value theorem" and other basic results of calculus. Dedekind's proof is simplicity itself: Given a family of real numbers, which is to say, of cuts, with an upper bound, just take their union to get a least upper bound. Dedekind remarks that, in teaching introductory calculus, to save time it is better not to go into such things, but just rely on geometric intuition. But his cut construction found its way into introductory college textbooks, beginning with the second edition of G. H. Hardy's *Pure Mathematics* (1914).

It should be noted that on this construction the rational numbers $\mathbf{Q}$ are not literally included in the real numbers $\mathbf{R}$, but only an isomorphic copy, with the rational q replaced by the cut consisting of all rationals $p < q$. Reconstructions tend to distinguish natural number 2, the integer $+2$, the rational $+2/1$, and the real 2.000000. Some symbolic computation programs do the same, but ordinary mathematical usage does not. But ordinary mathematical usage is admitted to include many an "abuse of language."

5.3 Peano Postulates

What are (for debatable historical reasons) called the *Peano postulates* for the natural numbers, zero, and successor, denoted $\mathbf{N}$, 0, and S, read as follows:

(P1) $0 \in \mathbf{N}$

(P2) $S : \mathbf{N} \to \mathbf{N}$

(P3) $\forall x \in \mathbf{N} \ (S(x) \neq 0)$

(P4) $\forall x \in \mathbf{N} \ \forall y \in \mathbf{N} \ (S(x) = S(y) \supset x = y)$

(P5) $\forall X \subseteq \mathbf{N} \ ((0 \in X \wedge \forall x \in \mathbf{N}(x \in X \supset S(x) \in X)) \supset \forall x \in \mathbf{N} \ (x \in X)).$

Here (P5) is called the *principle of mathematical induction*, and may be restated as follows. Call X *inductive* if 0 is in X and X is "closed under" S, meaning $S(x)$ is in X whenever x is in X. Then any inductive set contains all natural numbers. Applied to the set $\{x \in \mathbf{N} | \Phi(x)\}$, we can prove a condition holds $\Phi(x)$ for all natural numbers by proving (i) *the zero or base case*, that it holds for 0; and (ii) *the successor or inductive step*, that it holds for $S(x)$ assuming *the induction hypothesis* that it holds for x. This method is ubiquitous in mathematics.

Before we can do number theory we need to have the operations of addition, multiplication, and exponentiation, as well as the relation of order. Addition can be characterized by the following *recursion equations*:

(1) $x + 0 = x$
(2) $x + S(y) = S(x + y)$.

Laying down such equations is called *definition by recursion*, but since $+$ occurs on both sides of (2) we do not have here a definition comparable to those exhibited in tables so far, which make it possible to replace the defined symbol anywhere by an expression not involving it. But Dedekind showed how to make an honest definition of recursive specifications, in several stages. First, fix x, and call a function *good* for x if we have the following, for all y:

(3) $0 \in \operatorname{dom} f \wedge f(0) = x$
(4) $S(y) \in \operatorname{dom} f \supset (y \in \operatorname{dom} f \wedge f(S(y)) = S(f(y)))$.

A good f behaves like the function taking y to $x + y$ as far as it goes. One can show by induction that if g and h are good and y is in the domain of both, then $g(y) = h(y)$. The zero case is immediate, since (3) specifies the value for 0 . The successor step is immediate given the induction hypothesis that $g(y) = h(y)$, since (4) specifies the value for $S(y)$ given the value for y.

Second, one can show by induction that for every y there is a good f with y in its domain. For the zero case take $\{(0, x)\}$, a function with domain $\{0\}$ satisfying (3), which also satisfies (4) "vacuously" since 0 is not a successor by (P3). For the successor step, given the induction hypothesis that there is a good f with y in its domain, if $S(y)$ is already in the domain of f we are done. Otherwise, consider $g = f \cup \{(S(y), S(f(y)))\}$, a function since f is one and $S(y)$ is not in its domain, which satisfies (3) since f does, and satisfies (4), since f does and $S(y)$ is not the successor of anything but y by (P4). Thus the conditions "for some good f with y in its domain $f(y) = z$" and "for every good f with y in its domain $f(y) = z$" are equivalent, and for each y there is a unique z such that it holds. Replacement allows us to form the set of all pairs (y, z) satisfying the condition to give a function f_x with $f_x(0) = x$ and $f_x(S(y)) = S(f_x(y))$. Do this for all x, and replacement then allows us to form the set $\{f_x | x \in \mathbf{N}\}$, and union allows us to form the desired function $+$.

We can define $x \leq y$ to hold if $x + z = y$ for some z. We can define multiplication and exponentiation by recursion equations analogous to (1) and (2). Given these definitions, we can establish the basic laws of arithmetic by induction. For instance, for the associative law for addition the zero case and successor step look like this:

$$x + (y + 0) = x + y = (x + y) + 0$$

$$x + (y + S(z)) = x + S(y + z) = S(x + (y + z))$$
$$= S((x + y) + z) = (x + y) + S(z).$$

The other laws are not hard *if taken in the right order* (which is not always obvious). But we are not yet done.

To accommodate applications to counting finite sets we need to define what it is for set X to have a natural number x as the number $\#X$ of its elements. We can then define X to be *finite* if we have $\#X = x$ for some x in $\mathbf{N}$. The definition that works has $\#X = x$ if there is a bijection between X and the set of natural numbers $< x$. We need also to connect the recursive definitions of the arithmetic operations with the combinatorial characterizations of those same operations, familiar from school. In the case of addition, for the combinatorial character- ization we consider the union of two disjoint sets, or equivalently but more artificially, of disjoint copies of two sets. In the case of multiplication, it is the Cartesian product. In the case of exponentiation – where up-arrow notation will be typographically more convenient that superscript notation – it is the set of functions from one set to another. Table 13 shows what we need. To prove the needed equalities using induction we start by showing that if $\#X = x$ and $y \notin X$, then $\#(X \cup \{y\}) = S(x)$ and work from there.

It "only" remains to obtain from the axioms of set theory an $\mathbf{N}$ and a 0 and an S satisfying the Peano postulates. All we need is a set X with a function from X to X that is an injection but not a surjection. For then we can pick any element not in its range and call it zero, while calling the function itself successor, and

Table 13 Combinatorial Characterizations

Operation	Characterization	Definition of Set Operation
$\#X + \#Y$	$= \#(X \oplus Y)$	$= \#(\{(0, x) \| x \in X\} \cup \{(1, y) \| y \in Y\})$
$\#X \cdot \#Y$	$= \#(X \otimes Y)$	$= \#\{(x, y) \| x \in X \wedge y \in Y\}$
$\#X {\uparrow} \#Y$	$= \#(X \Uparrow Y)$	$= \#\{f \| f : Y \to X\}$

we will have (P3) and (P4). We can then define a subset Y of X to be *inductive* if it contains 0 and is closed under S, and trivially X itself will be inductive, and hence the family of inductive sets nonempty. We may then take **N** to be the intersection of this family, which can easily be seen to be itself inductive, giving (P1) and (P2). As for (P5), it will essentially have been made true by the mere definition of **N**. Contrary to a widespread opinion, classically expressed in Poincaré (1905/1983), intuition is not needed, but only logic, to obtain mathematical induction – given set theory. For set theory does, with its axiom of infinity, supply us with a set and a nonsurjective injection of the kind required, one for which $0 = \emptyset$ and $S(x) = \{x\}$.

This formulation is Zermelo's. There is an equivalent alternative due to John von Neumann (1923/1967), with $0 = \emptyset$ but $S(x)$ defined not as $\{x\}$ but as $x \cup \{x\}$, abbreviated x'. That $x' = y'$ implies $x = y$ is less obvious than that $\{x\} = \{y\}$ implies $x = y$, but not too hard to prove using foundation. (For x' has an *epsilon-maximal* element, one of which all its other elements are elements, namely x, and it cannot have any other such $y \neq x$, since that would give $x \in y \in x$, contrary to foundation. If $x' = y'$, their epsilon-maximal elements, x and y, must be the same.) Where the Zermelodic definition makes a natural number the singleton of its immediate predecessor, the Neumannian makes it the set of *all* its predecessors: $1 = \{0\}$, $2 = \{0, 1\}$, $3 = \{0, 1, 2\}$, and this allows us to give the simple definition $\#X = x$ if there is a bijection between X and x. It also has the advantage of generalizing to the transfinite, as will be seen later. Other mathematicians never think about whether $2 = \{1\}$ or $2 = \{0, 1\}$, but set theorists adhere to the latter. There are also variations on these constructions in which infinity is *not* needed for the theory of natural, integral, or rational (as contrasted with real and complex) numbers.

Set theory provides a framework for the rigorous development of all mathematics. Each branch, group theory or field theory or whatever, is concerned with some special kind of set-theoretic structure, groups or fields or whatever, and the "axioms" of the theory are merely the definition of the class of structures in question. Often ZFC is described as a "foundation" for mathematics, but such a description is questionable. To accommodate all mathematics, ZFC includes some assumptions more open to doubt than what would be needed just to accommodate arithmetic. Hence, incorporating arithmetic into set theory is not placing it on a firmer foundation. Rather, it is placing it in a context where it can interact with other branches of mathematics, with a common standard of proof. That is accomplishment enough.

6 Infinities

With the number systems available for examples, we are where Cantor was when he took off into the transfinite. Intuitively, their *equivalence type* is what items equivalent in some way thereby have in common, as lines in the plane that are parallel have in common their direction. Cantor understood the *power* or *cardinal* $\|A\|$ of a set A to be its equivalence type under equipollence or equinumerosity $\approx$, and the *order type* $|A|$ of an ordered set **A** to be its equivalence type under isomorphism $\cong$. He called the order types of wellorders *ordinals* and the cardinals of wellorderable sets *alephs*. He never identified such items with sets, but of his account of what they are (mental items created by acts of selective inattention), the less said the better. A good deal can be established while remaining silent about such issues.

6.1 Cardinals

Cantor defined $\|A\| = \|B\|$ if there is a bijection $f : A \to B$. He defined sum and product and power, $+$ and $\cdot$ and $\uparrow$ as in Table 13 of §5.3. In particular, with $\aleph_0 = \|N\|$, $2_0^\aleph$ is the cardinal of all zero-one sequences, or equivalently of all sets of natural numbers. He defined $\|A\| \leq \|B\|$ if there is an injection $f : A \to B$, equivalent to there being a C with $\|A\| + \|C\| = \|B\|$ (Consider $C = B - \operatorname{ran} f$.) Many of the laws proved by induction for natural numbers hold for cardinals generally, by proofs directly from the definitions. For instance, the associative and commutative laws for addition follow from the corresponding laws for union, and ultimately disjunction. Other laws fail badly, notably cancellation:

$$x + z = y + z \supset x = y \qquad z > 0 \wedge x \cdot z = y \cdot z \supset x = y.$$

Counterexamples include these:

$$\aleph_0 = \aleph_0 + \aleph_0 = \aleph_0 \cdot \aleph_0 \qquad 2_0^\aleph = 2_0^\aleph + 2_0^\aleph = 2_0^\aleph \cdot 2_0^\aleph.$$

For products, the result about $\aleph_0$ follow from the codability of a pair (m, n) of naturals by the single natural $2^m \cdot (2n + 1)$, and the result about $2^{\aleph}{}_0$ then follows using general laws of exponents: $2_0^\aleph \cdot 2_0^\aleph = 2_0^{\aleph + \aleph}{}_0 = 2_0^\aleph$. Failure of cancellation means that there is no subtraction or division for Cantor's transfinites, which have nothing to do with the supposed infinitesimals of prerigorous calculus. For antisymmetry of $\leq$, even without cancellation we still get the law.

Cantor–Bernstein Theorem If $\|A\| \leq \|B\|$ and $\|B\| \leq \|A\|$ then $\|A\| = \|B\|$.

Textbook proofs generally presuppose that the apparatus of natural numbers and definition by recursion has already been set up in a set-theoretic context before this topic is broached. This is partly for historical reasons: the earliest proof (Bernstein's) was found when set theory was still being pursued taking the traditional numbers systems for granted, without thought of redeveloping arithmetic from set-theoretic axioms. And it is partly for pedagogical reasons: that proof has the advantage of lending itself to illustration by a picture. But there are also advantages to having a proof more from first principles, such as could be used to develop the general theory of cardinals *before* the finite cardinals or natural numbers are singled out for special attention. Let me outline such a proof (due to Zermelo, building on Dedekind) as a series of exercises for the reader, since it is not very often presented elsewhere:

(1) Let $g: A \to B$ and $h : B \to A$ be injections.
Let $B^* = h[B] \subseteq A$ and $C = h[g[A]] \subseteq B^*$ and $f(g \circ h)^{-1}: A \to C$.
Show that f is a bijection.

(2) Define $G: \mathcal{P}(A) \to \mathcal{P}(A)$ by $G(X) = (A - B*) \cup f[X]$.
Show that $G(X) \subseteq G(Y)$ whenever $X \subseteq Y$.

(3) Show that $\{X \subseteq A | G(X) \subseteq X\} \neq \varnothing$, implying that $Z = \cap \{X \subseteq A | G(X) \subseteq X\}$ exists.

(4) Show that $G(Z) \subseteq Z$. Then show that $G(Z) = Z$.

(5) Define $k: A \to B^*$ by $k(x) = f(x)$ if $x \in Z$ and $= x$ otherwise. Show that k is a bijection.

(6) Let $g^* = k \circ h^{-1}$. Show that $g^*: A \to B$ is a bijection.

This result is used in computations. For $2^{\aleph_0} = \|\mathcal{P}(\mathbf{N})\|$ and $\mathbf{c} = \mathbf{R}$ it is easier to show $\|\mathbf{R}\| \leq \|\mathcal{P}(\mathbf{N})\| \leq \mathbf{R}$ than to show $2^{\aleph_0} = \mathbf{c}$ directly.

Cantor's diagonal argument, used to prove $\mathbf{c}$ uncountable, generalizes. Given a set K of cardinal κ and a family of subsets of K indexed by a set of cardinal κ, say K itself, there is a subset of K left out of the family, namely, if $\{X_k : k \in K\}$ is the family, $\{k | k \notin X_k\}$ is left out. This shows that $2^{\kappa} > \kappa$ for all κ, giving indefinitely many larger and larger cardinals.

6.2 Order Types

By order, understand in the present discussion *strict* order. The *reverse* of an order $<$ is the order $>$. The *sum* and *product* of orders $\mathbf{A} = (A, R)$ and another order $\mathbf{B} = (B, S)$ are the orders on $A \oplus B$ and $A \otimes B$, respectively, given as follows.

$$(i,x) < (j,y) \quad \text{if } (i = j = 0 \wedge xRy) \vee (i = 0 \wedge j = 1) \vee (i = j = 1 \wedge xSy)$$

$$(a,b) < (c,d) \quad \text{if } bSd \vee (b = d \wedge aRc)$$

Table 14 Counterexamples

Order Type	Looks Like
$1 + \omega$	$(0, 0), (1, 0), (1,1), (1,2), (1, 3), \ldots$
$\omega + 1$	$(0, 0), (0, 1), (0, 2), (0, 3), \ldots (1,0)$
$2 \cdot \omega$	$(0, 0), (1, 0), (0, 1), (1, 1), (0, 2), (1, 2), (0, 3), (1, 3), \ldots$
$\omega \cdot 2$	$(0, 0), (1, 0), (2, 0), (3, 0), \ldots (0, 1), (1, 1), (2, 1), (3, 1), \ldots$

Thus the sum puts a copy of **A** before a copy of **B**, while the product orders pairs in *reverse dictionary* order, first by their second components, and if these are the same, then by their first components. The *reverse* $\rho*$ of the order type ρ of **A** is the order type of the reverse of **A**, and similarly for sums and products. It can be checked that these notions are "well-defined": If two orders are isomorphic, having the same type, the same is true of their reverses, and similarly for sums and products. If we give the order types of the usual orders on naturals **N** and integers **Z** the names ω and π, then $\pi = \omega^* + \omega$.

Some of the usual laws hold, by extensions of the proofs used in the case of cardinals. This includes the associative laws. Other laws that held for cardinals fail for order types, including the commutative laws. Examples in Table 14 illustrate the point, showing $1 + \omega = 2 \cdot \omega = \omega$, while $\omega + 1$ is different, having a last element with no immediate predecessor, and $\omega \cdot 2$ is different, having an element with no immediate predecessor, but no last element.

Characterizations of the order types ω and λ of **N** and **R** are at least implicit in Dedekind. The characterization of the order type η of **Q** is a famous theorem of Cantor. To state these results, we need a few more notions pertaining to orders beyond those of wellorder and continuous order. An order is *dense* if whenever $x < y$ there is a z with $x < z < y$, and a subset Z of A is *dense* in the order if whenever $x < y$ there is a $z \in Z$ with $x < z < y$. Thus **Q** is dense in **R**. An order with a countable dense subset is called *separable*. Thus **R** is separable. By contrast, an order is *discrete* if every element x but the least (if any) has an *immediate predecessor*, a $y < x$ with no z between, and every element x but the last (if any) has an *immediate successor*, a $y > x$ with no z between.

The characterizing properties of the traditional orders are as in Table 15. Only Cantor's famous "back and forth" argument for η will be given here. (The same argument, going only "forth" and not "back," shows that every countable order is isomorphic to a suborder of **Q**.)

So let **A** and **B** both have the properties indicated for η in the table. We may take one of them to be the rationals. Since A and B are both countable, we can fix

Philosophy and Logic

Table 15 Characterizations of Order Types

Type	Properties
ω	wellordered, discrete, no greatest element
η	countable, dense, no least or greatest element
λ	continuous, separable, no least or greatest element

an enumeration of each, which need have nothing to do with the order relations $\leq_A$ and $\leq_B$. Call f a *partial isomorphism* if it is a function from a finite subset of A to a finite subset of B that preserves order.

Lemma If f is a partial isomorphism, for any a in $A -$ dom f there is a b in $B -$ ran f such that $g = f \cup \{(a, \; b)\}$ is a partial isomorphism.

Informally, "we can add any element we like to the domain of a partial isomorphism." For the proof, to preserve order, if a is $<$ all elements of dom f in **A**, we need b to be $<$ all elements of ran f in **B**. If a is between two elements a^*, a^{**} of dom f in **A**, we need b to be between $b^* = f(a^*)$ and $b^{**} = f(a^{**})$ in **B**. If a is $>$ all elements of dom f in **A**, we need b to be $>$ all elements of ran f in **B**. In each of the three cases a suitable b is available because **B** has no least element, or because **B** is dense, or because **B** has no greatest element. For definiteness, we may take for b whatever suitable element comes earliest in the fixed enumeration of B. Essentially the same proof shows we can add any element we like to the range of a partial isomorphism. To prove Cantor's characterization theorem we go back and forth in steps, at even steps adding to the domain, at odd steps to the range, getting a sequence of partial isomorphisms with larger and larger domain and range until A and B have been exhausted, when putting everything together we get an isomorphism between **A** and **B**.

A problem of Mikhail Suslin concerning λ also deserves mention. Separability, the existence of a countable set containing at least one element from every open interval, implies the nonexistence of an uncountable family of nonoverlapping open intervals. Can the latter *replace* separability in the characterization? *Suslin's hypothesis* (SH) is that it can. Information about the status of SH will be provided later.

6.3 Ordinals

We now take up von Neumann's approach to ordinals and alephs. A set x is *transitive* if every element of an element is an element, $\cup x \subseteq x$, or equivalently, every element is a subset, $x \subseteq \mathcal{P}(x)$. A (*von Neumann*) *ordinal* is a transitive set on which $\in$ is a strict wellorder. Then *isomorphism* with an ordinal α means isomorphism with this order $(\alpha, \in)$. The development of the theory of ordinals is facilitated by foundation (although feasible without it), using the following.

Ordinal Criterion If x be transitive and suppose $\in$ is connected on x. Then x is an ordinal.

Proof: Foundation implies irreflexivity of $\in$. We then get transitivity of $\in$ on x because for elements of x if $w \in v \in u$, foundation precludes having $u = w$ or $u \in w$, and connectedness leaves $w \in u$ the only alternative. So $\in$ is a strict order on x, which foundation, with the existence of epsilon-minimal elements, then says is a wellorder.

Ordinal Transitivity Let x be an ordinal and u an element of x. Then u is an ordinal.

Proof: The argument just given shows that u is transitive, and connectedness of $\in$ is inherited from x.

Ordinal Connectedness Let x and y be ordinals. Then either $x \in y$ or $x = y$ or $y \in x$.

This is a more substantial result. Here is the proof in outline as exercises for the reader:

(1) Show that if $y - x \neq \emptyset$, and z is an element thereof, then $x \cap y \subseteq z$.
(2) Show that if $y - x \neq \emptyset$, and z is an epsilon-minimal element thereof, then $x \cap y = z$.
(3) Show that we cannot have both $y - x \neq \emptyset$, and $x - y \neq \emptyset$.
(4) Show that if $x \neq y$, either $y \subseteq x$, implying $x \cap y = y$, or $x \subseteq y$, implying $x \cap y = x$.
(5) Show that either $x \in y$ or $x = y$ or $y \in x$.

Given ordinal transitivity and connectedness, the argument for the criterion shows that $\in$ is a strict wellorder relationship on ordinals, and accordingly with ordinals we write $\in$ and $<$ interchangeably, and each ordinal becomes the set of all ordinals less than it. By the foregoing, if contrary to fact the ordinals formed a set, it would be an ordinal, and the largest ordinal, a result known as the Burali–Forti paradox. (A "paradox" because example (2) below shows there can be no largest ordinal.)

Ordinal Examples
The zero, $0 = \emptyset$, is an ordinal, the least.
The successor, $x' = x \cup \{x\}$, of an ordinal x is an ordinal, the least $> x$.
The supremum $\sup X = \cup\, X$, of a set X of ordinals is an ordinal, the least $\geq$ all elements of X.

Proofs are left as exercises, unpacking definitions. As for notation, $1 = 0', 2 = 1'$, ... and $\omega = \sup\{0, 1, 2, \ldots\}$, the least *limit* ordinal, or ordinal neither zero nor a successor. We reserve lowercase Greek α, β, γ for ordinals. A function whose domain is an ordinal α is called an α-*sequence*, and if its value for $\beta < \alpha$ is denoted x_β, the sequence may be denoted $(x_\beta | \beta < \alpha)$, although, in the case of a finite sequence, we will not distinguish those of length two from ordered pairs, and will use the usual notation for pairs, triples, and so on; similarly with an ω-*sequence* such the zero-one sequences in the diagonal argument.

Ordinary finite induction for natural numbers has an analogue, transfinite induction for ordinals.

Induction If for, all α, $\Phi(\alpha)$ holds provided $\Phi(\beta)$ holds for all $\beta < \alpha$, then $\Phi(\alpha)$ holds for all α.

Proof: The proviso says there is no *least* α for which $\Phi(\alpha)$ fails, so by the wellorder property than can be none at all.

In proofs by induction, the proof of the proviso often breaks up into three cases according as α is zero, a successor, or a limit. As simple application we have the following.

Lemma Let $\S$ be an order-preserving operation on ordinals. Then for all α we have $\alpha \leq \S\alpha$.

Proof: The zero case is trivial. In the successor case, having $\alpha \leq \S\alpha$, since $\alpha < \alpha'$ we must have $\S\alpha < \S\alpha'$, whence $\alpha < \S\alpha'$, whence $\alpha' \leq \S\alpha$ because α' is the *least* ordinal $> \alpha$. The limit case is left as an exercise.

Corollary No ordinal is isomorphic to any smaller ordinal.

For if $f: \alpha \to \beta$ were an isomorphism with $\beta < \alpha$, we would have $f(\beta) < \beta$, whereas by the lemma we have $\beta \leq f(\beta)$.

Along with induction we have *ordinal* or *transfinite* recursion. We can specify $\alpha + \beta$ as follows:

α	if $\beta = 0$
$(\alpha + \gamma)'$	if $\beta = \gamma'$
$\sup \{\alpha + \gamma | \gamma < \beta)$	if β is a limit.

This can be turned into an honest definition using induction as was done for natural numbers in §5.3 (defining a *good* function, and so on). Multiplication and exponentiation can be similarly introduced. And some ordinary laws can be proved by induction, usually with the zero and successor cases being just as for natural numbers. With other ordinary laws, the limit case cannot be pushed through, and we have a refutation by counterexample, for instance:

$$1 + \omega = \ \sup \ \{1 + n | n < \omega\} \ = \omega < \omega' \ = \omega + \ 1.$$

The inductive definitions of addition and multiplication can be connected with Cantor's notions of addition and multiplication for order types in general, in much the same way the inductive definitions were related to combinatorial characterizations for the natural numbers. One more important connection remains:

Comparison Lemma Every strict wellorder $\mathbf{A} = (A, \ <_A)$ is isomorphic to some ordinal.

Uniqueness of the ordinal, which may be called the *order type* of the wellorder, follows from the corollary. For the proof, suppose $\mathbf{A}$ is a counterexample. $B \subseteq A$ is an *initial segment* of $\mathbf{A}$ if $x \in B$ whenever $x <_A y \in B$. We define an order-preserving operation f from ordinals to an initial segment B, thus: If $f(\beta)$ has been defined for $\beta < \alpha$, its range cannot be all of A, else we would have an isomorphism between α and $\mathbf{A}$; so let $f(\alpha)$ be the $<_A$ least element of A that is $>_A f(\beta)$ for any $\beta < \alpha$. We get an injective operation from all ordinals into A, hence a bijective operation from all ordinals onto some $B \subseteq A$. Replacement guarantees the existence of $\{f^{-1}(a) | a \in B\}$, but this is the set of all ordinals, which cannot exist! The Burali–Forti paradox, originally a misguided objection to Cantor, becomes a useful lemma. Here is another.

Hartogs' Lemma For every set X there is an ordinal α with no surjection $f : X \rightarrow \alpha$.

For the proof, any surjection $f \colon X \rightarrow \alpha$ gives rise to an equivalence relation $f(x) = f(y)$ on X and hence a partition of X, as well as a strict wellorder R on the cells of the partition, given by $[x]R[y]$ iff $f(x) < f(y)$; and the order type of this partition is α. Every strict wellorder on the cells of a partition of X belongs to $\mathcal{P}(\mathcal{P}(X) \otimes \mathcal{P}(X))$, and separation lets us form the set Y of all such R, and then replacement lets us form the set Z of all order types of elements of Y. If β is the least ordinal greater than all those in Z, called the *Hartogs' number* of X, then there can be no surjection $f \colon X \rightarrow \beta$. Note that neither can there be an injection $g \colon \beta \rightarrow X$. The importance of his lemma from Hartogs (1915) seems to have been only rather belated recognized.

6.4 Alephs

While it can be proved by mathematical induction that no finite ordinal is equinumerous with any smaller one, and that there is 'up to isomorphism' only one way to order a finite set, already there are many non-isomorphic ways of ordering the set of positive integers, as exhibited in Table 16, which should be compared with Table 14 of §6.2.

Table 16 Non-Isomorphic Wellorders

Order Type	Wellorder of Positive Integers
ω	1, 2, 3, ...
$\omega + 1$	2, 3, 4, ... 1
$\omega \cdot 2$	1, 3, 5, ... 2, 4, 6, ...
ω^2	1, 3, 5, ... 2, 6, 10, ... 4, 12, 20, ...

With ordinals, if there is a surjection $f : \alpha \to \beta$, there is an injection $g : \beta \to \alpha$ sending $y < \beta$ to the least $x < \alpha$ with $f(x) = y$. Conversely, given an injection g we get a surjection f sending $g(y)$ to y and anything not in ran g to 0. An *initial ordinal* is one for with no surjection from a smaller ordinal onto it, or equivalently no injection from it into a smaller ordinal. We denote the Hartogs' number of an ordinal α by α^+. We can define by recursion an indexing of all infinite initial ordinals by $\omega_0 = \omega$, $\omega_{\alpha+1} = \omega_\alpha^+$, and $\omega_\alpha = \sup \{\omega_\beta \mid < \alpha\}$ at limits. An *aleph* is the cardinal of a wellorderable set. Alephs may be identified with initial ordinals: $\aleph_\alpha = \omega_\alpha$. But with aleph notation + and · denote cardinal operations, with omega notation, ordinal operations. The most important fact about the arithmetic of alephs is that $\aleph_\alpha = \aleph_\alpha + \aleph_\alpha = \aleph_\alpha \cdot \aleph_\alpha$. This is proved by induction. Considering here only the result for multiplication, the zero case we know. In the successor case, suppose $\aleph_\alpha = \aleph_\alpha \cdot \aleph_\alpha$ and $\beta = \alpha'$ so $\aleph_\beta = \aleph_\alpha^+$. To show $\aleph_\beta = \aleph_\beta \cdot \aleph_\beta$ it suffices to show that we can wellorder $\omega_\beta \otimes \omega_\beta$ in order type ω_β, which means that the number of pairs $<$ any given one is $< \aleph_\beta$. For this it will be enough that the predecessors any pair (γ, δ) all come from $\zeta \otimes \zeta$ for some $\zeta < \omega_\beta$, since the number of ordinals $< \zeta$ is $\leq \aleph_\alpha$ and the number of suitable pairs then $\leq \aleph_\alpha \cdot \aleph_\alpha = \aleph_\alpha$. The order that works puts $(\gamma, \delta) < (\mu, \nu)$ if one of the following holds.

max $(\gamma, \delta) < $ max (μ, ν)

max $(\gamma, \delta) = $ max (μ, ν) and $\gamma < \mu$.

max $(\gamma, \delta) = $ max (μ, ν) and $\gamma = \mu$ and $\delta < \nu$.

The order type ξ of the predecessors of (γ, δ) in this order may be considered single ordinal *code* for the ordinal pair. The limit case is left as an exercise. Sierpinski (1958) is a compendium of further results on cardinal and ordinal arithmetic.

Let us tie up a loose end. For any x its *transitive closure* $x\dagger$ is the union of the sets $f(n)$ defined inductively by $f(0) = \{x\}$ and $f(S(n)) = \cup f(n)$. It contains x, the elements of x, the elements of elements, and so on, and is a transitive set, and one included in any transitive set containing x. Ordinal induction has a generalization, epsilon induction:

Induction If for, all x, $\Phi(x)$ holds provided $\Phi(y)$ holds for all $y \in x$, then for all x, $\Phi(x)$ holds.

For suppose $\Phi(x)$ fails. Then $\{y \in x\dagger | \neg\Phi(y)\}$ is non-empty and by foundation has an epsilon minimal element y. Since $x\dagger$ is transitive, $x\dagger$ contains all $z \in y$, and by minimality, $\Phi(z)$ holds for all such z, while failing for y, contrary to hypothesis.

We can define by ordinal recursion $V(0) = \varnothing$, $V(\beta + 1) = \mathcal{P}(V(\beta))$, and $V(\alpha) = \cup \{V(\beta) | \beta < \alpha\}$. It can be proved by ordinal induction that $V(\beta) \subseteq V(\alpha)$ when $\beta \leq \alpha$, and all $V(\alpha)$ are transitive and indeed *supertransitive*, meaning $y \in V(\alpha)$ whenever $y \subseteq x \in V(\alpha)$. It can then be proved by epsilon induction that for every x there is an α with $x \in V(\alpha)$. For if for each $y \in x$ there is a β and therefore a *least* β with $y \in V(\beta)$, replacement implies the existence of the set of all such least β for $y \in x$. If α is their sup, then $x \subseteq V(\alpha)$ and $x \in V(\alpha')$. These $V(\alpha)$ should be recognizable as the boxes of the cumulative hierarchy in Table 4 of §2.2. The least α with $x \in V(\alpha')$ is called the *rank* rk(x) of x. The intuitive 'justification' of the axioms of set theory in §2.2. in effect shows the following.

$$\text{rk} (\{a, b\}) = \max(\text{rk}(a), \text{rk}(b)) + 1$$
$$\text{rk}(\cup x) \leq \text{rk}(x)$$
$$\text{rk}(\mathcal{P}(x)) = \text{rk}(x) + 1$$
$$rk(\omega) = \omega.$$

If E is an equivalence relationship, we can define the *truncated* equivalence class $\ll x \gg$ of x to be the set of y with xEy of minimum possible rank, so that for any z, if xEz then $\text{rk}(z) \leq \text{rk}(y)$. (It will be a subset of $V(\text{rk}(x)')$, existing by separation.) These truncated equivalence classes have the one mathematically important property of equivalence types, namely, that xEy if $\ll x \gg = \ll y \gg$. And so we can take as set-theoretic surrogates for order types of nonwellorders and cardinals of nonwellorderable sets the truncated equivalence classes with respect to isomorphism and equinumerosity. This approach is often called "Scott's trick" after Dana Scott, who originated it. (The advantage of the von Neumann identifications in the case of wellorders and wellorderable sets is that they make the order type to be a specific wellorder of that type, and the cardinal to be a particular set equinumerous with the given one.)

7 The Axiom of Choice

The axiom of choice (AC), of which no use has been made thus far, has both inconspicuous and conspicuous applications, sometimes in providing counter-examples to conjectures, sometimes in proving positive results, including Zermelo's premier application to proving that **R** is wellorderable.

7.1 Weak and Full Choice

A *countable union* of sets of some kind means simply the union of a countable family of sets each of that kind. Two fundamental theorems of Cantorian theory read as follows.

Theorem A A countable union of countable sets is countable.
Theorem B If A is infinite, then $\|A\| \geq \aleph_0$.

To prove (A) one might argue thus: Let the family be $\{A_n | n \in \mathbf{N}\}$, and let $A_n = \{a_{mm} | m \in \mathbf{N}\}$. Then the union is the set of a_{mm} for $(m, n) \in \mathbf{N} \otimes \mathbf{N}$, and we can use the coding of pairs of naturals by single naturals to get an enumeration.

To prove (B), one might argue thus: Let a_0 be any element of A. Since A is not finite, it has an element a_1 other than a_0. Again since A is not finite, it has an element a_2 other than a_0 and a_1. And so on. $\{a_m | m \in \mathbf{N}\}$ is a subset of A of size $\aleph_0$.

Both arguments are fallacious, and the theorems cannot be proved in ZF = ZFC minus AC. The argument for (A) assumes we have a specific enumeration for each A_m, and requires (CC) below, applied to $F(n) =$ the family of all enumerations of A_n. That for (B) requires (DC) below, applied to the relation R that holds between an ordered m-tuple of elements of A and an extension to an ordered $(m + 1) - tuple$ of elements of A whose last element is different from its first m.

Countable Choice (CC) If F is a function with domain $\mathbf{N}$ with $F(n) \neq \emptyset$ for all n, then there is a function f with domain $\mathbf{N}$ with $f(n) \in F(n)$ for all n.
Dependent Choice (DC) If R is a relation on a set X such that for all $x \in X$ there exists a $y \in X$ with xRy, then there is a function $f: \mathbf{N} \to X$ with $f(n)Rf(n + 1)$ for all n.

DC implies that there is an infinite descending sequence in any order that is not a wellorder. It is left to the reader to show that CC is implied by DC, and DC by the following:

(**AC**$*$) Let I be any nonempty set, and X the family of its nonempty subsets. Then there exists a function $\varepsilon: X \to I$ with $\varepsilon(A) \in A$ for all A in X.

Such an ε is called a *choice function* for *I*. AC* is implied by AC as originally formulated. (The converse is also true, and left as an exercise.) For consider the set of pairs (A, a) with $a \in A \in X$ and the partition of that set in which the cell of (A, a) is the set of pairs (A, b) with same first component. Then a selector for this partition will be the required ε. A contrast between the special cases CC or DC of choice and full strength AC or AC* of choice is that applications of the latter tend to be conspicuous, those of the former, easily overlooked.

With full AC, theorem A can be generalized to any aleph κ, to show that a union of $\leq$κ sets each of size $\leq$κ has size $\leq$κ. An aleph λ is called *regular* if a union of $< \lambda$ each of size $< \lambda$ has size $< \lambda$, so the result just stated can be restated as saying that the successor $\lambda = \kappa^+$ of any aleph κ is regular. Theorem A itself says $\aleph_1$ is regular.

Henri Lebesgue's theory of "measure" (1902) involved an early application of Cantor's ideas. The theory shows how to define notions of length, area, and volume for a family of curves, surfaces, and solids, called *Lebesgue measurable*, extending far beyond those of Euclidean geometry. One can define, for instance, for an extensive family of subsets of the unit circle, a reasonable notion measure or "total length" with these features:

(1) The measure of the whole circle is its circumference 2π.
(2) If one set can be carried to another by rotation, they have the same measure.
(3) The measure of the union of a countable family of pairwise disjoint sets is the sum of the measures of the individual sets.

Lebesgue's work left open whether such a notion of measure μ could be defined for *all* subsets of the circle. Giuseppe Vitali (1905) answered this question negatively by a conspicuous application of AC. Call points on the circle equivalent if one can be carried to the other by a rotation of a rational fraction of a full 360°. Apply AC to obtain a selector *S* with one point in each cell of the induced partition. Since the whole circle is the union of the rotations of *S* through rational angles, of which there are only countably many, by (1) and (3) the sum of the measures of these sets should be 2π. But by (2) the measures of these sets should all be equal. And the sum of denumerably many copies of the same quantity $\mu(S)$ must be either zero (if $\mu(S) = 0$) or infinite (if $\mu(S) > 0$). Vitali's counterexample has many elaborations, of which the most famous is the *Banach–Tarski paradox*: a solid ball can be disassembled into a finite number of pieces which can be rotated, translated, and reassembled into two balls the same size. See Blumenthal (1940) for an early account in English.

7.2 Equivalents of Choice

AC also has positive consequences, notably the following crucial result of Zermelo.

Wellordering Principle (WO) Every set is wellorderable.

Proof: Given a set A, fix a choice function ε for A, and let e be any nonelement of A. Define by recursion an operation f assigning to ordinals elements of A as follows: If $f(\beta)$ has been defined for $\beta < \alpha$, consider $B = \{f(\beta)|\beta < \alpha\}$. Let $f(\alpha) = \varepsilon(A - B)$ if $A - B \neq \varnothing$, and $f(\alpha) = e$ otherwise. By Hartogs' lemma there must be an α for which the latter case applies, else we would have an injection of the Hartogs' number of A into A. For the least such α we have $A = \{f(\beta)|\beta < \alpha\}$ and we can wellorder A by setting $f(\gamma)Rf(\beta)$ iff $\gamma < \beta$.

That conversely WO implies AC* is almost immediate. To get a choice function for a set I having a wellorder R on I, let $\varepsilon(A) =$ the R least element of A, for any nonempty $A \subseteq I$. Many positive applications of AC can be made without bringing in apparatus pertaining to wellorders (which many mathematicians would prefer to avoid) by use of the following.

Zorn's Lemma (ZL) A partial order in which every chain has an upper bound has a maximal element.

Proof: Given the partial order $\mathbf{P} = (P, \leq_p)$, fix a choice function ε for P, and let e be any nonelement of A. Define by recursion an order-preserving operation from ordinals to $\mathbf{P}$ as follows.

$f(0) = \varepsilon(P)$

$f(\beta') = \varepsilon(\{p \in P|p >_p f(\beta)\})$ if $f(\beta)$ is not maximal, and $= e$ otherwise

$f(\alpha) = \varepsilon(\{p \in P|p \text{ is an upper bound to the chain } \{f(\beta)|\beta < \alpha\}\})$ at limits

Apply Hartogs' lemma as in the proof of WO.

Conversely, ZL implies AC. Given a partition X of a set I, let P consist of all *partial selectors*, or subsets of I containing *at most* one element of each cell, partially ordered by inclusion. It is easily checked that every chain has an upper bound (its union), and that a maximal element must be a selector (else we could add one element from any cell missed).

Assuming AC, all cardinals are alephs, and so $\kappa \cdot \kappa = \kappa$ for all κ. Alfred Tarski showed this result implies AC. See Gillman (2002). There are endless other known equivalents. See Rubin and Rubin (1970).

8 Topics in Higher Set Theory

The material presented so far includes the basics of what would be covered (with less philosophical commentary and with a good deal of mathematical detail here left to the reader spelled out for the student) in any of the several fine introductory textbooks on various levels that are available. Halmos (1960) covers less, Hrbacek and Jech (1999) more. This includes about as much of set theory as working mathematicians in most branches of mathematics are acquainted with. There is a great deal more to set theory than that, but just as Euclid's *Elements* leaves out such advanced topics as we find in the works of Apollonius and Archimedes, so this Element will have to pass over a vast amount of material in silence, or with only few allusions. And while some ideas of the proofs of the results that *do* get cited in the remainder of this work will be indicated, there will usually be even less detail than in the proofs or proof sketches up to this point. And while the names of many of the principal contributors to the subject will be mentioned, because the earlier of their original papers are often in French or German, and the later often would require years of graduate study to be able to read, citations merely for purposes of documenting historical attributions will be suppressed, except for the most important landmarks.

Higher set theory comprises three areas of study: (i) *descriptive set theory*, concerned with the reals and special sets thereof, or roughly with $V(\omega + 1)$; (ii) *continuum theory*, concerned with abitrary sets of reals, or roughly with $V(\omega + 2)$, (iii) *combinatorial set theory*, concerned with arbitrary sets of arbitrary elements, and with higher $V(\alpha)$. (The V notation is as in §6.4.) They have been listed in order of decreasing direct relevance to other branches of mathematics. Indirect relevance is another matter, since the three areas turn out to be connected with each other in deep ways it will take some time to bring out. All three abound in questions that cannot be settled on the basis of the axioms of ZFC alone, so that many of the most important results to be reported belong to the so-called *metamathematics* of set theory, being theorems about what isn't a theorem of ZFC. Axioms beyond ZFC eventually get brought in, and here the different characters of the three areas come out. Axioms arguably expressing the thought that the universe of sets is maximally "high" (so-called *large cardinal* axioms) have turned out to tell us almost everything about area (i) and almost nothing about area (ii). Axioms arguably expressing the thought that the universe of sets is maximally "wide" (so-called *forcing* axioms) are having great impact on area (ii), but less on area (iii). But before taking up these advanced matters, we need some sample results from each of the three areas.

8.1 Descriptive Set Theory

The development of geometry within algebra and analysis and thence set theory involves identifying linear or plane points with elements of $\mathbf{R}$ or $\mathbf{R} \otimes \mathbf{R}$. Once it is clear we are dealing with mathematical "spaces" and not physical space, we can freely introduce Euclidean spaces of any dimension, and non-Euclidean spaces of any kind. The theory of special sets of points on the real number line is called *descriptive set theory*, but its results extend to a wider range of spaces treated, for instance, in the classic Kuratowski (1966), and called *Polish spaces*.

Still, we begin with $\mathbf{R}$. Its countably many *basic* sets are open intervals $]a,\ b[$ defined as $\{x \in \mathbf{R} | a < x < b\}$ with rational endpoints a, b. (Often in the literature, the simple notation (a, b) is used for the open interval, but we have been using that simple notation for the ordered pair, which we have had much more occasion to mention. Either way $[a,\ b]$ denotes the closed interval $\{x \in \mathbf{R} | a \leq x \leq b\}$.) Two intervals, $]a,\ b[$ and $]c,\ d[$ are *separate* if $b < c$ or $d < a$, so they neither overlap nor abut. In the real plane $\mathbf{R} \otimes \mathbf{R}$, similar definitions can be made starting from rectangles. The *projection* of a planar set $A \subseteq \mathbf{R} \otimes \mathbf{R}$ is the linear set $B \subseteq \mathbf{R}$ that would be called dom A when thinking about A as a relation, namely, the set of first components of ordered pairs in A. Further sets of interest are classified in *point classes* as defined in the adjoining Tables 17 and 18.

Using such facts that countable unions of countable sets are countable, and the DeMorgan and Distributive laws for indexed families, it can be shown that

Table 17 Lower Point Classes

Class	Definition
open	unions of basic sets
closed	complements of open sets
F_σ	countable unions of closed sets
G_δ	countable intersections of open sets
Borel	sets obtainable from the above by further countable intersection and union

Table 18 Higher Point Classes

analytic	projections of Borel sets
coanalytic	complements of analytic sets
PCA	projections of coanalytic sets
CPCA	complements of PCA sets
projective	sets obtainable from the above by further projection and complementation

the intersection or union of two (and hence of finitely many) sets in any of these classes is in the class, that G_δ sets are complements of F_σ sets, that open sets are F_σ and closed sets are G_δ, that countable unions of F_σ sets are F_σ and countable intersections of G_δ sets are G_δ, and so on. Such basic theorems would be early exercises in a textbook.

Even sets in the lowest point-classes can be by ordinary standards quite complicated. They include all the "fractals" pictured in coffee-table books. Yet since there are only countably many basic sets, there are only **c** open sets, and this extends to projective sets. Since there are 2^c arbitrary subsets of **R**, this means descriptive set theory is concerned with only a small fraction. Yet sets in the indicated point classes include all those ordinarily encountered in analysis, apart from pathological counterexamples like Vitali's.

Higher theorems about a point class Γ are of two kinds: A *regularity* theorem says that each set in Γ is "nice" in some way (Lebesgue measurability being one kind of "niceness" especially important for other branches of mathematics). A *structural* theorem says that different sets in Γ are "nicely related" in some way. For instance, sets C, D are said to *reduce* sets A, B if the following relationships hold:

$$C \subseteq A \quad D \subseteq B \quad C \cup D = A \cup B \quad C \cap D = \varnothing,$$

The *reduction principle* for Γ says any pair of sets in Γ is reduced by some pair of sets in Γ.

Sample Structural Theorem The reduction principle holds for F_σ sets.

Proof sketch: Let A be the union of closed A_i and B the union of closed B_i for $i \in \mathbf{N}$. Let C consist of those x such that for some i, x is in A_i but not in B_j for any $j < i$, and D of those x such that for some i, x is in B_i not in A_j for any $j \leq i$. The elements of $A \cup B$ that "get into A no later than into B" are in C, while those that "get into B sooner than into A" are in D. Reduction is easily verified, while C and D being F_σ can be verified using the fact that finite unions and intersections of closed and open sets are simultaneously F_σ and G_δ.

A *perfect* set P is one that (i) is closed and (ii) has no isolated points. Here (i) implies that if every basic set containing a point x meets P, then x is in P, while (ii) means that any basic set U that meets P contains at least two distinct points x and y of P. From this it follows that U includes two separate basic sets V and W that both meet P (V containing x and W containing y), which moreover may be taken to be as short as desired in length. So we can obtain basic sets U_0 and U_1 of length $< \frac{1}{2}$ that both meet P, then separate basic subsets U_{00} and U_{01} of U_0 and U_{10} and U_{11} of I_1 of length $< \frac{1}{4}$ that all meet P, and so on. For any infinite zero-one sequence, say $\sigma = (0, 1, 1, \ldots)$ the intersection of U_0 and U_{01} and U_{011}

and U_{0111} and so on will be a singleton $\{x_\sigma\}$ such that every basic set containing x_σ meets P, making x_σ an element of P, while separateness of the different Us means that distinct σs give distinct x_σs. Hence P contains as many elements as there are zero-one sequences, and we have sketched a proof that *any perfect set has cardinal* **c**.

A set A has the *perfect set property* if it is either countable or contains a perfect subset. This implies that A is either countable or of cardinality **c**, but is a stronger statement, since AC implies there exist pathological sets of size **c** without perfect subsets. To sketch a proof, since there are only **c** perfect sets, with AC we can wellorder them in a sequence P_α indexed by ordinals $\alpha < $ **c**, so that each has $< $ **c** predecessors. And then we can inductively choose x_α and y_α distinct from each other and from all x_β and y_β with $\beta < \alpha$, and both in P_α, since at stage α only fewer that **c** points will have been chosen, while P_α has **c** to choose from. In the end, the set of all x_α will have size **c**, but include no perfect set P_α, having left out y_α.

Now consider a closed set C and go back to Cantor's construction with which we began in §1.1, successively discarding isolated points, taking derived sets indexed by ordinals. Each time a point is discarded, it belongs to a basic set with no other point in it, and we can say that whole basic set is discarded with the point. Since there are only countably many basic sets to discard, the process can only go on for countably many stages, and can only discard a countable set C_0 of points. If nothing is then left, then $C = C_0$ is countable. If anything is left, it is a perfect set. We have sketched the proof of the following.

Cantor–Bendixson Theorem Any uncountable closed set is the union of a countable and a perfect set.

In particular, closed sets have the perfect set property. But then so does any union of a countable family of closed sets, since if each set in the family is countable, so is their union, while if any contains a perfect subset, the union contains it, too. So we have the following.

Sample Regularity Theorem Every F_σ set has the perfect set property.

The Polish and Russian schools between the world wars created classical descriptive set theory, obtaining regularity and structural theorems much stronger than our samples, extending to much larger point classes: notably, the Lebesgue measurability (and an analogous *Baire property*) of all analytic and coanalytic sets, and the reduction principle (and a stronger *uniformization* principle) for PCA sets. But then progress halted. The reason why will emerge later.

8.2 Continuum Theory

A couple of negative general theorems about arbitrary sets of reals have already been given: the theorem that not all sets have the perfect set property, and that not all are Lebesgue measurable (to which it could be added that not all have the property of Baire). Such theorems have at least the value for other branches of mathematics of warning the mathematician not to try to do the impossible. And such negative results are, in a sense, what motivates descriptive set theory: If a regularity property cannot be established for all sets, then let us look at larger and larger classes for which it can be established. And in order to have still sets with a given regularity property while performing various operations creating new sets from old, we will want structural theorems saying that various classes are closed under various operations.

One significant open question at this level has been mentioned in §6.2, the status of the *Suslin hypothesis* (SH). But the main question in the theory of arbitrary sets of reals is the *continuum hypothesis* (CH). Actually, there are two propositions so named, as follows.

There is no cardinal λ with $\aleph_0 < \lambda < 2^{\aleph}_0$ $2^{\aleph}_0 = \aleph_1$.

The second implies the first, and the first implies the second if c is an aleph, so assuming AC, as we will here, the two are equivalent. CH was conjectured by Cantor, and placed first on his 1900 list of mathematical problems for the new century by Hilbert. Like AC, CH has many equivalents and interesting conse-quences (see Sierpinski, 1956). The main alternatives to CH considered have been that $c = \aleph_2$ and that c is a *fixed point of the alephs*, a κ such that $\kappa = \aleph_\kappa$. One isolated result proved early is *König's theorem* that $c \neq \aleph_\omega$. But after this there were a several of decades of lack of progress.

The reason why emerged in the middle 1900s. *Gödel's First Incompleteness* theorem tells us any reasonably strong consistent mathematical axiom system T will leave some Ψ *undecidable*, neither provable nor disprovable. (By contrast, an inconsistent axiom system can prove *anything*. For a contradiction $\Phi \wedge \neg\Phi$ implies Φ, but also $\neg\Phi$ hence $\neg\Phi \vee \Psi$, which is $\Phi \supset \Psi$ while Φ and $\Phi \supset \Psi$ imply Ψ, whatever it may be.) *Gödel's Second Incompleteness* theorem gives a specific example, telling us that Con(T), the assertion that T is consistent, will be unprovable (if true). But the first *natural-looking* specific mathematical statement shown to be undecidable by ZFC was CH.

Kurt Gödel (1940) and Paul Cohen (1966) proved respectively that ZFC cannot disprove and cannot prove CH (assuming ZFC is consistent). Their precise results are stated in Table 19. Note that, per the second incompleteness theorem, the results are *relative* ("if this is consistent, so is that") rather than

Table 19 Undecidability "Metatheorems"

Author	Metatheorem about CH	Metatheorem about AC
Gödel	$\text{Con}\,(\text{ZFC}) \supset \text{Con}\,(\text{ZFC} + \text{CH})$	$\text{Con}\,(\text{ZF}) \supset \text{Con}\,(\text{ZF} + \text{AC})$
Cohen	$\text{Con}\,(\text{ZFC}) \supset \text{Con}\,(\text{ZFC} + \neg CH)$	$\text{Con}\,(\text{ZF}) \supset \text{Con}\,(\text{ZF} + \neg \text{AC})$

absolute ("such-and-such is consistent"). Gödel's method of proof, with the so-called *inner model* of *constructible sets*, establishes relative consistency not only for CH but for a generalization GCH to be introduced in §8.3. Cohen's method of proof, that of so-called *forcing*, can be used to give a different proof of relative consistency for CH as well as a proof of ¬CH. Both methods have been found to have innumerable other applications and are absolutely central to the ongoing work of set theorists today. While it would be infeasible to attempt to expound these methods in any detail in a work such as this – they are not covered even in the most thorough introductory-level texts – it will prove possible to give some idea of their nature later.

Meanwhile let it be noted that *either* method can be used to prove the relative consistency of ¬SH, as was done by Ronald Jensen using Gödel's method and by Thomas Jech and independently by Stanley Tennenbaum using Cohen's method. Further, Robert Solovay, among many other important early applications of Cohen's method, used it in joint work with Tennenbaum to prove the relative consistency of SH.

Although these methods originated to deal with problems at the level of the theory of arbitrary sets of reals, they have also applications at other levels. In particular, John W. Addison, using Gödel's work, showed that regularity theorems cannot be extended to higher point classes than the classical workers between the world wars had handled, while Azriel Levy, using Cohen's method, showed the same for structural theorems, thus explaining the impasse that had been reached by the Polish and Russian schools.

All this means that, if regularity and/or structural theorems are to be obtained for higher point classes, or if the status of SH and/or CH is ever to be settled, new axioms beyond ZFC will be needed. Gödel and Cohen drew opposite philosophical conclusions from this situation, Cohen doubting there was any fact of the matter about whether CH is true, and Gödel (1947) advocating a search for new axioms to prove or (as he thought more likely) disprove it. Thus far, however, no hypothesis settling the size of **c** has acquired the status of an accepted axiom, the way AC, after some resistance, eventually did. But a vigorous research program continues, of which more later.

8.3 Combinatorial Set Theory

There are two propositions called the *generalized continuum hypothesis* (GCH):

There is no cardinal λ with $\kappa < \lambda < 2^{\kappa}$ for any κ $2^{\aleph_{\alpha}} = \aleph_{\alpha+1}$ for all α.

As with CH, the second implies the first and the first implies the second assuming AC; but, in fact, we can simply say they are equivalent, since a striking result of Waclaw Sierpinski tells us the first version *implies* AC. (See Gillman 2002.) GCH is the main question of interest about the arithmetic of arbitrary cardinals, and perhaps as such the main question of interest in the theory of arbitrary sets of arbitrary elements. But it is hardly the only question of interest, there being, to begin with, a large body of results constituting an infinitary combinatorics, related to transfinite arithmetic as finite combinatorics (beginning with the highschool topic of counting permutations and combinations) is related to ordinary arithmetic. As this subject may be unfamiliar even at the level of the countable, let alone higher cardinals, let us begin with sample theorems at that level.

First, a *tree* is a partial order $(P, \leq)$ with a minimum element, in which the predecessors of any element are wellordered. The elements are called *nodes*, the minimal one the *root*, the order type of the predecessors of a node its *level*, and the supremum of nodes' levels the tree's *height*. We will be concerned for the moment only with trees of height $\leq \omega$. A infinite *branch* through such a tree is a chain containing one node at level n for each $n < \omega$.

König's Infinity Lemma Any finitely branching tree of infinite height has an infinite branch.

Proof: If the tree has infinite height, it has infinitely many nodes, all above its root x_0. Since x_0 has only finitely many nodes immediately above it, by the "pigeon-hole principle" at least one such node x_1 must have infinitely many nodes above it. Similarly, at least one node x_2 immediately above x_1 must have infinitely many nodes above it, and so on. Then $\{x_0, x_1, x_2, \ldots\}$ is a branch.

Second, for any set X of more than two elements, $[X]^2$ denotes the set of two-element subsets of X. A *two coloring* for X is a partition of $[X]^2$ into two cells. We may think of the elements of X as dots with the segments connecting any pair of them colored red or blue. A *homogeneous set* is a subset of Y of X such that $[Y]^2$ is included in a single cell of the partition. All dots in Y are connected with the same color.

Infinite Ramsey's Theorem Any two coloring of an infinite set has an infinite homogeneous set.

Proof: Consider the hypothesis (H) *Any infinite subset of X contains an element red connected to infinitely many other elements of that subset.* First assume (H) holds. Let $X_0 = X$ and take an element a_0 of X_0 red connected to infinitely many elements of X_0. Let X_1 be the set of elements of X_0 red connected to a_0. Take an element a_1 of X_1 red connected to infinitely many elements of X_1. Let X_2 be the set of elements of X_1 red connected to a_1. And so on. $\{a_0, a_1, \ldots\}$ is a red homogeneous set. Now assume (H) fails, so there is some infinite subset Y_0 of X such that any element thereof is red connected to only finitely many elements thereof, and hence is blue connected to infinitely many. Take an element b_0 of Y_0 blue connected to infinitely many elements of Y_0. Let Y_1 be the set of elements of Y_0 blue connected to b_0. And so on, to obtain a blue homogeneous set.

Finite Ramsey's Theorem For every finite m there is a finite n such that any two coloring of a set of size n has a homogenous set of size m.

(For $m = 3$ we may take $n = 6$. Connect six dots red and blue and there will be a red or a blue triangle.) Proof sketch: Suppose for some m there is no suitable n. We form a finitely branching tree of configurations. At the root, there is just one dot. Above it at the next level are two configurations, both adding a second dot, but differing as to the color, red or blue, of its connection with the first. Above each are four configurations, each adding a third dot, but differing in the color pattern of its connections, red-red or red-blue or blue-red or blue-blue with the first two. And so on. Now go through the tree removing configurations in which there is a homogeneous set of size m (all configurations above one so removed being removed along with it). Since there is no suitable n, there will still be nodes at level n for all n. By König's lemma, the tree must have an infinite branch. But from such a branch, we obtain a configuration of *infinitely many* dots with no homogeneous set of size m and hence certainly no infinite homogeneous set, contrary to the infinite Ramsey theorem.

Both versions of Ramsey's theorem can be generalized, to consider partitions of n-membered subsets rather than two-membered, and to allow m colors rather than two. The proof just given of the finite theorem is an example of a route to a result about the finite with a detour through the infinite. There are any number of such proofs in mathematics, a famous one being the original proof by Pafnuty Chebyshev of *Bertrand's postulate* to the effect that there is a prime between any prime and its double, which used complex analysis. The proof of Fermat's theorem by Andrew Wiles makes use of especially complicated apparatus. Hilbert hoped it could be shown that detours through the infinite can always be avoided, and certainly they sometimes can. Ramsey's original (1930) and more difficult proof of his finite theorem involved no infinitistic moves. And Srinivasa Ramanujan and Paul Erdös have each given "elementary" – meaning in this context *noninfinitistic*, not *easy* – proofs of Bertrand's postulate. There remains hope also that someone, somewhere, sometime will obtain one for Fermat's theorem. But J. B. Paris and Leo Harrington found a version of the finite Ramsey theorem "with bells and whistles" for which they could show the detour through the infinite to be indispensable.

One large class of results about arbitrary sets of arbitrary elements consists of attempting to determine how far Ramsey's theorem can be generalized: For which cardinals κ, λ, μ, and natural numbers n, is it true that any partition of the n-membered subsets of a set K of size κ into μ classes will have a homogeneous set of size λ, a subset $L \subseteq K$ of that size all of whose n-membered subsets belong to the same class? This relationship is written $\kappa \to (\lambda)^n{}_\mu$. In this notation the basic version of Ramsey's theorem says $\aleph_0 \to (\aleph_0)^2{}_2$. Perhaps the best known further result of this type is that of Erdös and Richard Rado, according to which the relation holds for $\kappa = \mathbf{c}^+$ and $\lambda = \aleph_1$ and $\mu = \aleph_0$ and $n = 2$.

Issues about "partition calculus" are a prominent part of "infinite combinatorics" although hardly the whole. Before leaving the subject, let me list just a few more results, whose proofs would take us too far afield here, to indicate the variety of questions that arise in this area, and perhaps pique the interest of some readers. (Hrbacek and Jech have especially good coverage for an introductory text. See also Kunen (1977).)

Almost Disjoint Sets Call subsets of **N** *almost disjoint* if they have finite intersection. Then there is a family of size **c** of pairwise almost disjoint sets.

Dickson's Lemma Let k be a positive integer and consider a sequence of k-tuples of natural numbers $(a_{m1}, \ldots a_{mk})$ for $m \in \mathbf{N}$. Then there exist $m < n$ with $a_{mi} \leq a_{ni}$ for $i = 1, \ldots, k$.

The Δ System Lemma Let X be an uncountable family of finite sets of countable ordinals. Then there is an uncountable subset Y of X and a finite set a of countable ordinals such that $b \cap c = a$ for all b and c in Y.

Fodor's Lemma Let f be a function from countable ordinals to countable ordinals with $f(\alpha) < \alpha$ for all $\alpha > 0$. Then there is a β such that $f(\alpha) = \beta$ for uncountably many α.

9 Metamathematics of Set Theory

Since the first development of non-Euclidean geometry, the standard way of proving consistency has been by constructing models, and the novelty in Gödel's and Cohen's work consisted precisely of new methods of model construction. Now since the existence of a model implies consistency, we cannot prove in ZFC the existence of a model for all of ZFC (provided ZFC is consistent, a parenthetical proviso left tacit henceforth). But there provably are models for large fragments, especially among the $V(\alpha)$, sometimes called "natural" models. Before examining these we need to say what more precisely is meant by a "model," which will involve examination of what is meant by "truth" and related notions, dodging paradoxes connected with such notions since antiquity.

9.1 Truth

We may begin with a modern, specifically set-theoretic paradox. Since there are only countably many finite sequences of symbols from a finite alphabet, there are only countably many ordinals definable by finite expressions. But there are uncountably many ordinals, so there must be undefinable ones, and among these a least. But that one is definable as *the least undefinable ordinal*. Such is *König's paradox*. One response is that in speaking of definability we must say in what language, and if it is that of set theory, what the argument shows is that set-theoretic definability is not set theoretically definable. But if set theory is supposed to accommodate everything mathematical, ought it not to accommodate defining definability? The response "that's not mathematics, it's *meta*mathematics" underwhelms.

Better to focus on what *is* definable. If mathematical logic is to be accommodated like other branches of mathematics within set theory, the objects of the language L of set theory must be identified with sets of some kind. Well, proofs are finite sequences of formulas, and formulas are finite sequences of symbols, and *finite sequence* is already a set-theoretic notion, so it remains only to identify *symbols* with sets. Epsilon and equals, the bar and caret and wedge of negation and conjunction and disjunction, the universal and existential quantifiers, and opening and closing parentheses for punctuation may be identified with the pairs $(0, 1)$ through $(0, 9)$. We also need variables $x, y, z, \ldots$, and these can be identified with pairs $(1, 0), (1, 1), (1, 2), \ldots$. Once it is clear we are dealing with a mathematical "language" and not natural languages, there is no reason not to expand it indefinitely to a language adding a name $\underline{a}$ for every set a. The details of how to define such syntactic notions as substitution of one symbol for another when logic is reconstructed set theoretically need not detain us any more than how to define exponentiation when reconstructing analysis. It can be done, but not here.

The notion of *truth* is "semantic" rather than syntactic, and can*not* be expressed in L, since if it could, so could the derivative notion of definability: a is definable if there is some formula $\Phi(x)$ of L such that the sentence $\forall x(\Phi(x) \leftrightarrow x = \underline{a})$, identifying the item named $\underline{a}$ as the only one satisfying condition Φ, is true. And if the notion of definability could be expressed in L, we would have König's paradox. A notion of truth *in a model* is, however, express-ible in L, and will be key. A *model* for present purposes will be a structure

Table 20 Recursive Characterization of Truth

Clause	Definition		
$\in$	$M| = \underline{a} \in \underline{b}$	if	$a \in b$
$\neg$	$M| = \neg\Phi$	if	not $M| = \neg\Phi$
$\wedge$	$M| = (\Phi\wedge\Psi)$	if	$M| = \Phi$ and $M| = \Psi$
$\forall$	$M| = \forall x\Phi(x)$	if	$M| = \Phi(\underline{a})$ for all a in M

Table 21 Δ_0 formulas

Notion	Formula
$x = \varnothing$	$\forall y \in x \, (y \neq y)$
$x = \{y, z\}$	$y \in x \wedge z \in x \wedge \forall w \in x \, (w = y \vee w = z)$
$x = (y, z)$	$\exists u \in x \exists v \in x(u = \{y, y\} \wedge v = \{y, z\} \wedge x = \{u, v\})$
$x = \cup y$	$\forall u \in y \, \forall v \in u \, (v \in x) \wedge \forall v \in x \, \exists u \in y \, (v \in u)$
$x \subseteq y$	$\forall z \in x \, (z \in y)$
$x \subseteq \mathcal{P}(y)$	$\forall z \in x \, (z \subseteq y)$
x is transitive	$\forall y \in x \, \forall z \in y \, (z \in x)$
x is an ordinal	x is transitive $\wedge \, \forall y \in x \, \forall z \in x \, (y \in z \vee y = z \vee z \in y)$
x is a limit ordinal	x is an ordinal $\wedge \neg(x = \varnothing) \wedge \forall y \in x \exists z \in x \, (y \in z)$
$x = \omega$	x is a limit ordinal $\wedge \neg \exists y \in x \, (y$ is a limit ordinal$)$

$\mathbf{M} = (M, \in)$ with M transitive, but while model and underlying set should be distinguished in principle, "abuse of language" can be allowed in practice, and the key notion of a sentence (formula without free variables) Φ of the language $L(M)$ with names (only) for elements of M being true in the model will be called truth in M and written $M| = \Phi$. The accepted treatment derives from Tarski and Vaught (1956) based on earlier work of Tarski. To begin with, we characterize it recursively in the adjoining Table 20.

The clauses for $=, \vee, \exists$ are left to the reader. The characterizations provided by Table 20 can be made into an honest definition as was done for natural numbers in §5.3 (defining a *good* function, and so on). What is being defined is the function $\tau(\Phi) = 1$ or 0 according as Φ is true or false in M, for sentences Φ of $L(M)$. If we tried to imitate the construction to define simple *truth* (in the universe of set theory, not just a model) for a sentence we would need a function like τ but defined on all sentences however high the rank of items named in them. But these are too many to form a set. Yet we can go some way towards defining truth by restricting the logical complexity of the sentences involved. A

Δ_0 formula is one that can be abbreviated to contain only bounded quantifiers, universal and existential, $\forall y \in x$ and $\exists y \in x$ as defined in Table 7 in §2.2. Many notions can be expressed by such formulas, and a few are shown in the adjoining Table 21. One could add "*x* is a partition" and "*y* is a selector for *x*" and more, but not "*x* is countable" or "$x = \mathcal{P}(y)$," which require unbounded quantifiers, existential and universal, $\exists y$ and $\forall y$, respectively.

A crucial property of a Δ_0 sentences is *absoluteness*. If M_0 and M_1 are transitive and Φ a Δ_0 sentence of $L(M_0) \cap L(M_1)$, then $M_0| = \Phi$ iff $M_1| = \Phi$. For while with an *un*bounded universal quantifier, when evaluating it per clause (4a) in M_i one has to look for a possible exception throughout (although not beyond) M_i, and there may be one in M_0 but not M_i, by contrast with a *bounded* universal quantifier $\forall x \in \underline{a}$ one only needs to look at *elements of a* in M_0 and in M_i, and these are the same, namely *all* elements of *a*, by transitivity. Similarly with existential quantifiers. Thus a model cannot "make a mistake" about whether a Δ_0 sentence is true, about whether the item named $\underline{a}$ is or is not the empty set, or whether the item named $\underline{b}$ is or is not the unordered pair of those named $\underline{c}$ and $\underline{d}$, and so on down the list in in the table. We may therefore define Δ_0 truth (truth for Δ_0 sentences) as truth in some, or equivalently every, model containing all items named in the sentence.

A $\sum_1$ or Π_1 formula is a Δ_0 formula with an unbounded existential or universal quantifier out front, or a string of them (although in examples just one will be written). Suppose M_0 and M_1 are transitive with $M_0 \subseteq M_1$. If a $\sum_1$ sentence $\exists y \Phi(y)$ of $L(M_0)$ is true in M_0, then there is some "witness" b in M_0 such that $\Phi(\underline{b})$ is true in M_0, and $\Phi(\underline{b})$ being a Δ_0 sentence it will still be true in M_1, as then will be $\exists y \Phi(y)$. $\sum_1$ sentences "relativize up" from smaller to larger models, while similarly Π_1 sentences "relativize down." We may define $\sum_1$ truth (respectively Π_1 truth) as truth in *some* model (respectively *all* models). Continuing, adding alternate universal and existential quantifiers, we can define the *Levy hierarchy* of $\sum_n$ and Π_n formulas for all n, with truth notions for each. The truth definitions get longer as n gets larger. So, although every formula can be reduced to a logically equivalent formula that is $\sum_n$ using simple logical equivalences, and called $\sum_n$ in a generalized sense, we cannot use this fact to define truth, since we would have to combine the $\sum_n$ truth definitions into a single infinitely long definition.

Truth-in-a-model will imply real $\sum_1$ truth, and real Π_1 truth will imply truth-in-a-model, but not always conversely. A model may "think" something is the uncountable $\mathcal{P}(\omega)$, or family of *all* subsets of ω, when it is really only some countable family of subsets of ω, making this mistake because *all in the model* is not the same as *all*. As a consequence of a famous result of mathematical logic, the *Löwenheim-Skolem Theorem*, that any sentence or countable set of sentences has a model has a countable model. Applied to ZFC (assuming it has a model, which recall cannot be proved, since having a model implies consistency, which cannot be proved), this tells us that theorems about the existence of enormous uncountable sets have countable models, an observation often called *Skolem's paradox*. (See Skolem 1922/1967.) We have just seen the explanation, but some philosophers still worry how anything we say could guarantee that when we utter "the power set of omega" we are talking of the real $\mathcal{P}(\omega)$ and not a countable imposter of which the things we are saying happen to be true in some model. See Putnam (1980).

9.2 Inaccessible Cardinals and Their Status

By the informal phrase "large cardinal" set theorists mean a cardinal that towers above all smaller ones in something like the way the infinite towers over the finite. To be counted by set theorists as "large," a cardinal κ must be a *limit*, meaning that if $\lambda < \kappa$, then $\lambda^+ < \kappa$, and even a *strong* limit, meaning that $2^\lambda < \kappa$. It must also be regular, meaning that a union of $< \kappa$ sets of size $< \kappa$ has size $< \kappa$. A regular strong limit is called an *inaccessible* (because it cannot be reached from below by the most common methods of producing larger sets from smaller), and these are the smallest large cardinals, first considered by Zermelo (1930) and independently of him by Sierpinski jointly with Tarski. We will meet others later.

But let us first see what is special about inaccessibles.

The axiom of extensionality, in the form (2) of §3.1, $\forall x \forall y$ $(x \subseteq y \wedge y \subseteq x \supset x = y)$, is Π_1 and true, hence true in any model; and the same goes for foundation. The truth of other axioms in a model M requires some "closure" properties of the underlying set M. The truth of pairing in M requires that for every a and b in M there is a c in M that M "thinks" is $\{a, b\}$. But since this is one of those Δ_0 matters about which a model cannot be mistaken, this means that for every a and b in M, the real $\{a, b\}$ is in M, a feature called "closure under forming pairs." Similarly, the truth of union is equivalent to closure under forming unions. Infinity may be alternately formulated as $\exists(x = \omega)$, making its truth in M equivalent to presence of the real ω in M. While "partition" and "selector" are not in Table 21 of §9.1, these notions *are* Δ_0, implying choice will be true in M if every partition in M has a selector in M.

Power set requires that for every a in M there be some b in M that M thinks is $\mathcal{P}(a)$, which means that for all c in M, c is in b if c is a subset of a, which, in turn, means that really b is $\mathcal{P}^M(a) = \mathcal{P}(a) \cap M$. Closure under $\mathcal{P}^M$ is the criterion for truth of the axiom. If the model is *super*transitive, containing all subsets of its elements, then $\mathcal{P}^M(a) = \mathcal{P}(a)$ and the criterion is closure under $\mathcal{P}$. Separation is more complicated. By the *relativization* Φ^M of a formula Φ to M is meant the replacement of every quantifier $\forall x$ or $\exists x$ by $\forall x \in M$ or $\exists x \in M$. Truth of a sentence Φ in M is equivalent to truth of the Δ_0 sentence Φ^M. Truth in M of instance of separation for Φ requires for each a in M the presence in M of $\{x \in a | \Phi^M(x)\} \subseteq a$. A more than sufficient condition is supertransitivity.

The $V(\alpha)$ are supertransitive, and considerations of rank show that for limit α they are closed under formation of pairs, unions, and power sets, besides containing ω provided $\alpha > \omega$, and a selector for any partition, assuming AC. Thus for limits $> \omega$ we get a model of everything but replacement. A more than sufficient condition for replacement would be that any subset of M of the same cardinality as some element of M is an element of M. This condition is satisfied if $\alpha = \kappa$, an inaccessible cardinal, since it can be proved by induction for such a cardinal that $||V(\beta)|| < \kappa$ whenever $\beta < \kappa$ (using the strong limit property for successors and regularity for limits). Thus we have (a sketch of) a proof that *if κ is inaccessible, then $V(\kappa)$ is a model of* ZFC.

If we write IC for the hypothesis of the existence of an inaccessible, we have in outline proved IC $\supset$ Con(ZFC). This means that, in contrast to the situation with CH seen in Table 19 of §8.2, we cannot hope to prove Con(ZFC) $\supset$ Con(ZFC + IC), because then in ZFC + IC we could prove Con(ZFC + IC), contrary to the second incompleteness theorem unless ZFC + IC is inconsistent – and no one hopes *that*. This illustrates how large cardinal axioms are inherently risky. One cannot hope to prove even their *relative* consistency. Their greater inconsistency risk is (euphemistically) called greater *consistency strength*, and the larger the cardinal, the greater it is. The hypotheses get riskier and riskier until we come to the so-called *Reinhardt* cardinal, the assumption of whose existence Kenneth Kunen showed to imply a contradiction.

A brief polemical aside (see Maddy (2017) for nuance, Mathias (1992) for contrast): Saunders Mac Lane introduced *category theory* alongside group theory and so on as the theory of another class of set-theoretic structures. But enthusiasts have proclaimed it a rival to set theory as a "foundation." What seems to be involved here is a difference in understanding of the word "foundation," which anyhow has been avoided above in favor of "framework." An attempt was made to develop an axiom system for a category of all categories, to replace ZFC. It failed. A translation of ZFC into category-theoretic language has been developed, but the translation has not helped with major set-theoretic open problems. But to accentuate the positive, category-theoretic work of Alexandre Grothendieck, partly passed into folklore, led him to posit that the universe of set theory is made up of larger and larger "local" universes, which on examination prove to be precisely $V(\kappa)$ for inaccessible κ. Thus he found a way to motivate the Zermelo's assumption that there are arbitrarily large inaccessible cardinals.

Others have argued that the thought that the cumulative hierarchy is maximally "large" should be interpreted to suggest that anything we say in an attempt to describe just how large will inevitably be an understatement, not only true in the macrocosm of all sets, but "reflected" in some microcosm $V(\kappa)$. In something like this way, "intrinsic" motivations – as contrasted with "extrinsic" motivation provided by attractive consequences – has been claimed for inaccessible and some larger cardinals by Bernays, Levy, and others and others. Koellner (2009) is a sophisticated discussion of how far one can hope to go along such lines.

A less ambitious version of this idea is provable as a metatheorem about what is provable in ZFC, the *Levy Reflection Principle*. A transitive set M is Σ_1 *absolute* if every Σ_1 sentence of $L(M)$ that is true is true in M: For any Δ_0 formula $\Phi(x, y)$ of L, and any a in M, if $\exists y\Phi(\underline{a}, y)$ is true, so that there is a witness b somewhere for which $\Phi(\underline{a}, \underline{b})$ is true, then there is such a witness in M, making $\exists y\Phi(\underline{a}, y)$ true in M. Then we have the following:

Σ_1 **Reflection Principle** There exist arbitrarily large Σ_1 absolute $V(\alpha)$.

Given any γ, to any Δ_0 formula $\Phi(x, y)$ and any a in $V(\gamma)$ for which $\exists y\Phi(\underline{a}, y)$ is true, associate the least ordinal β such that there is a witness in $V(\beta)$. Replacement allows us to form the set of all such associated ordinals, and then take their supremum $\gamma^* > \gamma$. All Σ_1 sentences about elements of $V(\gamma)$ that are really true will be true in $V(\gamma^*)$. There may be Σ_1 sentences about elements of $V(\gamma^*)$ that are really true but not true in $V(\gamma^*)$, but we can repeat the process and take $\gamma^{**} > \gamma^*$ and $\gamma^{***} > \gamma^{**}$, and so on. Then the supremum α of these γs is Σ_1 absolute. More elaborate proofs extend the result to Σ_2, Σ_3, and so on. We can get a natural model $V(\alpha)$ of all the other axioms of ZFC plus as many instances of replacement as desired.

9.3 Inner Models and the Status of AC

While Gödel's original proof of the relative consistency of AC and CH is too complicated to reproduce here, for AC alone he later published a simplified proof, which can at least be outlined. AC has so far been used in our discussion of models where proving that AC is true in $V(\alpha)$, but nowhere else. In the present discussion, let the assumption of AC be dropped, and work in ZF, Zermelo–Fraenkel set theory *without* choice. Relativization Φ^Ψ to a formula Ψ is the result of each $\forall y \ldots$ being replaced by $\forall y(\Psi(y) \supset \ldots)$, and similarly for $\exists$, so that "for all sets" is reinterpreted as "for all sets for which Ψ holds," and similarly for "some." (Compare with the notion of relativization to a set M in §9.2.) Gödel's simplified proof the relative consistency of AC consisted in showing that for a suitable Ψ one can prove in ZF the relativization Φ^Ψ of each axiom Φ of ZF, as well as the relativization AC^{Ψ} of AC. Relativization preserves logical deducibility, and if a contradiction were deducible from the axioms of ZFC, one would be deducible from their relativizations, and hence from the axioms of ZF which imply those relativizations. It follows that if ZF is consistent, so is ZFC. But it will take some work to spell out what is Gödel's relativizing formula $\Psi(x)$, called HOD(x) and read "x is hereditarily ordinal definable."

A set a is *definable from an ordinal parameter* or *ordinal definable*, or OD for short if there is some formula $\Phi(x, y)$ of L and some ordinal α such that $\forall x(\Phi(x, \underline{a}) \equiv x = \underline{a})$ is true. This formulation, in terms of truth, is not expressible in L, although OD-in-a-model and Σ_n OD would be, using restricted notions of truth. Gödel's trick is to show that there is a (comparatively small) n such that anything OD is Σ_n OD, allowing (an equivalent of) OD to be expressed in L after all. To see this, suppose a is OD in the way indicated, by a Σ_k formula for some perhaps quite large k and some ordinal α. There are only countably many formulas of L and they can be assigned code numbers. Writing Ψ_j for the formula with code number j, we will have $\Phi = \Psi_i$ for some i. Apply the reflection principle to obtain a Σ_k absolute $\beta > \alpha$. We then have this:

(1) $V(\beta) \mid = \forall x(\Psi_i(x, \alpha) \equiv x = a)$.

In the proof of $\kappa \cdot \kappa = \kappa$ for all alephs κ, we saw how to code pairs of ordinals by single ordinals, and this obviously permits the coding of triples as well. Let γ code the triple (β, α, i). Then we have $\Theta(\underline{a}, \gamma)$ where this says:

(2) γ codes a triple (β, α, i) with $\beta > \alpha$ and $i < \omega$ such that (1) holds.

Then if $\Theta(y, z)$ is Σ_n, (2) shows that a is Σ_n OD from parameter γ. The least δ such that a is OD by this Σ_n formula Θ from parameter δ may be called the *defining ordinal* $\partial(a)$ of a. So a is OD if $\exists \delta(\delta = \partial(a))$, and this δ is necessarily unique if it exists. We may define a wellorder on OD sets by $a <_{OD} b$ if $\partial(a) < \partial(b)$. And the notions OD and $<_{OD}$ are expressible by formulas not much worse than Σ_n. Call a *hereditarily* OD or HOD if not only a itself but every other member of its transitive closure $a\dagger$ is OD. HOD(x) is Gödel's relativizing formula promised earlier.

The details of the proof that the relativization of each axiom of ZF to HOD is a theorem of ZF will not be given in this sketch. Note that HOD is transitive in the sense that if HOD(x) and $y \in x$, then HOD(y). One then makes use of the criteria from §9.2 immediately above for axioms holding relativized to a transitive set, adapted to relativization to the transitive condition HOD. For instance, one must show that if a and b are HOD, so is $\{a, b\}$. The only element of $\{a, b\}\dagger$ not in $a\dagger$ or $b\dagger$ is $\{a, b\}$ itself, so we need only worry about showing it is OD given that *a* and *b* are. The principle at work in showing this is that anything definable from OD sets (as a pair is definable from its elements) is OD. Since different ordinals α and β may be needed to define *a* and *b*, to define the pair we need to use the coding of pairs of ordinals by single ordinals. As for AC^{HOD}, it will come down to showing that any OD partition has an OD selector. The selector will be the one including the $<_{OD}$ least element of each cell. If the foregoing rather sketchy sketch does nothing else, it should illustrate the sophistication that Gödel brought to the metamathematics of set theory, which was then taken a step further by Cohen.

A by-product of this work is the observation that, because statements of number theory and finite combinatorics can all be formulated so as to mention only elements of $V(\omega)$, all of which are HOD, such a statement has the same meaning whether or not relativized to HOD. From this it follows that if it such a statement is provable assuming AC, it is provable without it. The same is known to hold for CH and any other hypotheses for which relative consistency has been proved. In contrast, large cardinal axioms, for which relative consistency cannot be proved, definitely make a difference. For instance, they imply Con(ZFC), which can be coded as a number-theoretic or finite-combinatorial statement. To be sure, as such it is rather artificial, and not something whose proof or disproof would be high up on any number theorist's or finite combinatorialist's research program. But for decades Harvey Friedman has been producing more and more natural-looking examples, though the long-await definitive exposition of his results, working title *Concrete Incompleteness*, must be awaited a bit longer, while preprints on particular aspects accumulate.

We can now say something about Gödel's proof of the consistency of CH (and GCH). A formula Θ amounts to, or the sets satisfying it collectively amount to – for both modes of expression are in use – an *inner model* of ZFC or some related set theory T if it shares three crucial properties established above for HOD.

Every ordinal satisfies Θ.
Θ is transitive: Every element of a set satisfying Θ satisfies Θ.
Every axiom of T remains true when quantifiers are relativized to Θ.

Gödel's original proof worked, not with the inner model HOD, but with another called L, whose definition is more delicate, giving more control of the outcome. It is, in particular, the *minimum* inner model: any sets present in it, that is, any sets satisfying its defining formula, must be present in any other inner model. The sets in L are called *constructible* and the inner model itself is called the *constructible universe*. Gödel shows that, in the constructible universe, the principle that every set is constructible, written V = L and called the *axiom of constructibility*, holds. (This is *not* a tautology: it says that if a set satisfies the formula defining constructibility, then it also satisfies that formula *when quan-tifiers are relativized to* L.) He then proceeds to show that $V = L$ implies AC, and CH, and indeed GCH. The facts have already been alluded to that Addison went on to prove that $V = L$ implies the existence of non-Lebesgue-measurable PCA and CPCA sets, and that Jensen later proved that it implies ¬SH (along with a lot of other combinatorial results), through an analysis of the so-called *fine structure* of L.

For another example of a proof by inner models, long before Cohen, Fraenkel, and Andrzej Mostowski in the 1920s and 1930s, considered the question of the consistency of ¬AC in the context of a modification ZFU of ZF that permits *Urelemente*, or *atoms* as they are sometimes called. In formulating ZFU, it is necessary to add a predicate meaning "is a set" and restrict the axiom of extensionality to sets, while asserting that non-sets or atoms *all* have no elements. In the Fraenkel–Mostowski work, we need a version of ZFU asserting that there are infinitely many atoms. They then prove Con(ZFU) implies Con(ZFU + ¬AC) by an inner model construction. Their methods can also be applied to distinguish various stronger and weaker variants of AC.

The key idea is that any permutation π of the atoms determines a permutation, by abuse of language also denoted π, of sets of atoms, and then of sets who elements may be atoms or sets of atoms, and so on up the cumulative hierarchy, the general pattern being $\pi(x) = \{\pi(y) \mid y \in x\}$. If $\Phi(x, y)$ is the formula $y \in x$, it is evident that for any a and b, the formula $\Phi(\underline{a}, \underline{b})$ is true if and only if $\Phi(\pi(\underline{a}), \pi(\underline{b}))$ is true, and this can be extended by induction on complexity to all formulas: in a slogan, "permutation preserves truth." We then define a set x to be of *finite support* (FS) if there is some finite set of atoms X such that any permutation that leaves the elements of X fixed, meaning $\pi(y) = y$ for all y in X, will also leave x fixed. Then just as Gödel moves from OD to HOD we move from FS to HFS, the inner model of sets x such that x itself, its elements, elements of its elements, and so on down are all of finite support. Then considerations of the kind used in the HOD proof show that HFS is an inner model of ZFU. But it cannot be a model of AC, since AC implies every set can be ordered (indeed, well ordered), but no order R of the whole infinite set of atoms can have finite support. For given any finite set X of atoms, take any atoms a and b not in it, with say $(a, b) \in R$, implying $(b, a) \notin R$, and consider the permutation π that just switches those atoms, so that π applied to the pair (a, b) is the pair (b, a). Then the π changes the truth $(a, b) \in R$ into $(b, a) \in \pi(R)$, implying $R \neq \pi(R)$. While Gödel's proof of consistency for CH involves further elaboration beyond his proof of consistency for AC, with Cohen the proof of the consistency of ¬AC is more complicated than his proof of consistency for ¬CH, since he must combine his machinery of forcing with the ideas of Fraenkel–Mostowski to establish for ZF what they establish for ZFU.

9.4 Forcing and the Status of CH

Any account of Cohen's forcing in a work at the elementary level of the present one will have to be even sketchier than the sketch of Gödel's inner models just given; yet something *can* be said that it is hoped will give at least a taste of the flavor of forcing constructions. While Gödel started with the universe V of all sets and contracted to an inner universe where CH is true, Cohen could not start with the universe V of all sets and expand to an outer universe where CH is false, since there is no room for an outer universe containing more sets than all the sets there are. His procedure had of necessity to be a bit more indirect. What he did was to start from a countable transitive model M of ZFC, and expand to an outer countable transitive model N where CH is false. Now ZFC, as already remarked earlier, cannot prove the existence of a model of ZFC, let alone of a countable transitive model. However, close inspection of Cohen's work shows that the truth of any finite subset of ZFC + ¬CH in N requires only the truth of some finite subset of ZFC in M, and this fact, together with some logician's tricks, permits one to conclude that if ZFC is consistent, so is ZFC + –CH. But in attempting to understand something about Cohen's method, it is best to concentrate on the model construction, and leave the trickery needed to extract a relative consistency proof to the logicians.

The central notions used in forcing are, like those used in formulating Zorn's lemma in §7.2, some further items to be added to the list of basic notions pertaining to partial orders given in §4.3. If $(P, \leq)$ is a partial order, a subset $D \subseteq P$ is called *dense* if for every p in P there is a $q \leq p$ in D. Two elements p, q of P are *compatible* if there is an r in P with both $r \leq p$ and $r \leq q$. A subset $A \subseteq P$ is an *antichain* if no two of its members are compatible, and P is ccc (or satisfies the *countable chain condition*) if it has no uncountable antichains. Finally, a subset $G \subseteq P$ is *generic* for a family F of dense sets if it satisfies the following:

Whenever $p \in G$ and $p \leq q$, then $q \in G$.
Any two elements of G are compatible.
For every $D \in F$, there is a $p \in G$ with $p \in D$ (so that $G \cap D$ is nonempty).

Note that for any *countable* $F = \{D_0, D_1, D_2, \ldots\}$ there exists a generic G. Just take any p_0 in D_0, then any $p_1 \leq p_0$ in D_1, then any $p_2 \leq p_1$ in D_2, and so on, and for G take the set of q such that for some n we have $p_n \leq q$. In particular, if P belongs to the countable model M, the set F of all its dense subsets *that belong to M* is countable, and there is a generic set G for it. This G, however, in general will *not* itself be in M. What Cohen shows is that there is a minimum countable transitive model $N = M[G]$ containing all the elements of M and G as well.

For his application to CH, or rather ¬CH, Cohen considers the ordinals α and β in M that M "thinks" are $\aleph_1$ and $\aleph_2$. Really they are both countable, and there is a surjection f from ω onto α and a surjection g from α onto β; it is just that there are no such f and g *in the model M*. For his set P of "forcing conditions," he takes all functions whose domain is a finite set of pairs (γ, m) with $\gamma < \beta$ and $m < \omega$, and whose values are all 0s and 1s. The partial order relation $\leq$ on P is just the reverse of set-theoretic inclusion $\subseteq$, so $q \leq p$ if the former is a function extending the latter to a larger domain, and two "conditions" p and q are compatible if there is no pair in the domain of both on which they give different values, so that their union is still a function. For any pair (γ, m), the set $D(\gamma, m)$ of p with that pair in its domain is dense: if (γ, m) is not already given a value by p, we can extend p to give it one. Similarly, for any $\gamma \neq \delta$ the set $E(\gamma, \delta)$ of p for which there is an m with $p(\gamma, m) \neq p(\delta, m)$ is dense. These dense sets are all in M, and Cohen takes a G generic for the family of all of them to form his $M[G]$. By the compatibility of all elements of a generic set, the functions in G fit together to form a big function g, which by the fact that G has nonempty intersection with each dense $D(\gamma, m)$ must have each (γ, m) with $\gamma < \beta$ and $m < \omega$ in its domain. Considering the $E(\gamma, \delta)$ it also follows that for any distinct $\gamma, \delta < \beta$ there is an m with $g(\gamma, m) \neq g(\delta, m)$. In other words, fixing γ and considering the infinite zero-one sequence $(g(\gamma, 0), g(\gamma, 1), g(\gamma, 2), \ldots)$ we get different sequences for different γ, and so a sequence of length β of distinct zero-one sequences. Since $\mathbf{c}$ is the number of zero-one sequences, and β was playing the role of $\aleph_2$, have we now shown the existence of a model with $\mathbf{c} \geq \aleph_2$?

Alas, not quite. For we need to show that β, which was the $\aleph_2$ of M, remains the $\aleph_2$ of $M[G]$, which in turn requires that α, which was the $\aleph_1$ of M, remains the $\aleph_1$ of $M[G]$; or, in other words, we need to show that no surjection from ω onto α or from α onto β has slipped into $M[G]$. This is the most technical part of the proof, and will be slighted here. Let it just be noted that it uses the fact that the partial order P is ccc (the proof of which uses the Δ system lemma from the end of §8.3).

The Solovay–Tennenbaum forcing for SH was much more complicated, essentially involving performing one Cohen-style extension after another in an infinite iteration. D. A. Martin and Solovay (1970) extracted from the proof a principle that has come to be called *Martin's axiom* (MA), producing a proof of the relative consistency of ¬CH + MA, as well as a proof that ¬CH + MA implies SH. MA says that if a partial order P has no uncountable antichain, then for any family F of fewer than $\mathbf{c}$ dense sets there exists a generic set G for F. Note that CH implies MA, since assuming CH "fewer than $\mathbf{c}$" amounts to "countably many," and we have seen that generic sets for countable families of dense sets always exist. Martin and Solovay report that, of the consequences of CH in the Sierpinski book, about half are provable from MA alone, and about half disprovable from MA + ¬CH, with a few left open. A particularly important example in the former category is the following. One of the most basic results of Lebesgue's theory of measure is that the union of countably many sets of measure zero still has measure zero, which assuming CH means that the union of fewer than c sets of measure zero still has measure zero. But this last result actually follows *without* CH just from MA.

Many further applications of MA have been found, not to mention applications of the more general method of forcing that produced it. (See Rudin (1977) and Burgess (1977) for examples: the volume from which these papers come emphasizes exposition for mathematicians who are *not* logicians or set theoreticians.) MA is the premier example of what is called a "forcing axiom" or principle saying that various kinds of thing that *could be made* true by Cohen's method *already are* true. (It was shown by Jouko Väänänen and Jonathan Stavi in the 1970s to follow from the principle that any statement of a certain form that can be made true by ccc forcing and cannot then be made false by further ccc forcing is true, which has been independently discovered or rediscoverd by others since.) Saharon Shelah initiated the study of stronger forcing axioms than MA + ¬CH, and in particular of ones that imply not just $c \neq \aleph_1$ but $c = \aleph_2$. The strongest principle in this direction has been called *Martin's Maximum* (MM), although its authors are not Martin but Matthew Foreman, Menachem Magidor, and Shelah. It has a wealth of consequences.

10 Large Cardinals and Determinacy

We turn next to the surprising connections that emerged, mainly in the 1970s and 1980s, between descriptive set theory, the theory of special sets of real numbers, and large cardinal theory, the loftiest part of the theory of arbitrary sets of arbitrary elements.

10.1 Beyond Inaccessibles

We have so far had occasion to mention (in §8.3) only the weakest large cardinal assumption, that of the existence of inaccessibles, which we called IC. But there is a zoo of large cardinals that are larger than inaccessibles, with more and stranger inhabitants than the zoo of fundamental particles in physics. Akihiro Kanamori (2003) provides a guide, which I cite as a one-stop source in preferences to the original papers of various authors. Four out of the many species of larger cardinals will have some degree of importance in what is to follow, and at least their names will be noted here in one place.

Weakly compact cardinals, introduced by Ersös and Tarski, are ones for which the analogue of the most basic form of Ramsey's theorem holds, one for which we have $\kappa \to (\kappa)^2_2$ in the notation of §8.3.

Measurable cardinals, introduced by Stanislaw Ulam, are perhaps worth a few more extended remarks. In many cases, it is possible to distinguish among the subsets of some infinite set X of some cardinality κ certain ones that are in some sense large, and certain others that are in a corresponding sense small, where the two classes have the following properties:

(1) The complement of a small set is large and the complement of a large set is small.
(2) A one-element set is small and an all-but-one-element set is large.
(3) Any set included in a small set is small and any set including a large set is large.
(4) Any union of $< \kappa$ small sets is small and any intersection of $< \kappa$ large sets is large.

For example, if X is the unit interval $]0,1[$ and κ the continuum **c**, then taking the Lebesgue measure 0 sets as small and the Lebesgue measure 1 sets as large, with have (1)-(3), and (4) also if MA is assumed. What we do not have in this example is this:

(5) Every set is either large or small.

For even apart from the question of the existence of nonmeasurable sets, there are many subsets of the unit interval of measure ½ or otherwise of intermediate size. If we do in some case get all of (1)-(5) we have in κ a *measurable cardinal*. The definition (1)-(5) could also be recast in terms of the *measure* function μ defined by $\mu(A) = 1$ if A is large and $\mu(A) = 0$ if A is small.

Woodin cardinals, named for their introducer Hugh Woodin, have a definition too complicated to be reproduced here.

Supercompact cardinals likewise. One of these is used in a relative consistency proof for MM.

As we go down the list, the cardinals are getting larger. It can be shown that if κ is weakly compact, then there are κ many inaccessible cardinals $< \kappa$. Similar relations obtain between weakly compact and measurable, and so on.

10.2 Infinite Games

We return to descriptive set theory to consider a rival to AC. By basic results in the Kuratowski book and elsewhere, many results established for any one Polish space will carry over to all others, and for many purposes it is easier to work with an alternative to **R**, either the *Baire space* $\mathbf{N^N}$ of infinite sequences of natural numbers, which looks just like the irrationals (using continued fraction expansions), or the *Cantor space* $2^{\mathbf{N}}$ of infinite zero-one sequences, which looks just like the famous Cantor middle-third set (the reals in the unit interval having a base-three expansion involving only digits 0 and 2). For any finite sequence s, of natural numbers or of zeros and ones, let $U(s)$ be the set of infinite sequences beginning like s. These are the basic sets of the Baire and Cantor spaces, comparable to open intervals with rational endpoints in **R**, in terms of which other point classes of Borel and projective sets can be defined.

The Polish school initiated study of *infinite games of perfect information* of the following kind. Let A be a subset of the Baire space. Two players, IN and OUT alternately pick natural numbers, each knowing at each stage the other's previous picks, thus generating an infinite sequence x in the Baire space. IN wins if $x \in A$, OUT wins if $x \notin A$. (IN goes first, like white in chess or black in go.) A *strategy* is a function from finite sequences of natural numbers to natural numbers. A player *follows* a strategy S in a play of the game if that player's move is always the output of S for input the opponent's sequence of previous moves. A strategy is *winning* for a given player if that player always wins when following it. Clearly *both* players cannot have winning strategies. If one or the other does, the game and the set A are called *determinate*. The Axiom of Determinacy (AD) asserts that all sets are determinate.

AD is known to imply certain regularity properties hold for *all* sets (such as Lebesgue measurability, for which see Mycielski and Swierczkowski, 1964). A notable such result is the following from Morton Davis (1964).

Davis Theorem Assuming AD, all sets have the perfect set property.

Proof-sketch: The proof will be given for the Cantor space, but the result holds for all Polish spaces. Given a subset A of the Cantor space, consider a game that is asymmetrical in the sense that the two players make different kinds of moves: alternately IN picks finite zero-one sequences and OUT picks single digits zero or one. Their picks are strung together to produce an element x, of the Cantor space, with IN or OUT winning according as x is or is not in A. AD implies the determinateness of this game. Now suppose IN has a winning strategy S. The element of A obtained when IN follows S is different for each sequence of plays by OUT, showing A has **c** elements. A closer look shows that the set of such elements is perfect. Now suppose OUT has a winning strategy and consider any element x of A. See how far the beginning of x can be divided up into alternating finite zero-one sequences followed by the single digit that would be given by S if OUT were following that strategy. The whole of x cannot be divided up in this way, since then it would represent the result of OUT following S for the whole course of play, which would mean that x is *not* in A. So suppose we get this far, then are stuck:

$$s_0, i_0, s_1, i_1, \ldots, s_n, i_n.$$

What is the next digit j_0 in x beyond those in this finite display of data? Since we are supposed to be stuck, it is *not* what S would tell OUT to play in response to IN's playing the empty sequence, but rather the opposite. What is the next digit j_1 after that? The *opposite* of what S would tell OUT to play if IN played the one-term sequence (j_0). What is the next digit j_3 after that? The *opposite* of what S would tell OUT to play if IN played the two-term sequence (j_0, j_1). And so on. All the digits of x are thus generated in terms of S from the finite pattern displayed. Since there are only countably many such patterns, there are only countably many elements x of A.

Since we have seen that assuming AC there are sets that do not have the perfect set property, the Davis theorem shows that AD contradicts AC, though the weaker DC is often assumed in conjunction with AD when considering its consequences. The existence of an indeterminate set could also be proved directly assuming AC, by a construction just like that used to prove the existence of a set lacking the perfect set property. The weaker *projective determinacy* (PD) asserts only the determinateness of projective sets. But that is enough to imply (by much the same proof) that all of *those* have the perfect set property. PD similarly implies other regularity properties (including Lebesgue measurability). How far can we go in proving determinateness for Borel and projective sets? Here is the first step:

Gale-Stewart Theorem All open sets are determinate.

Proof-sketch: We continue working with the Cantor space, but the argument would be the same for the Baire space. Let A be an open subset of the Cantor space, meaning a union of basic sets $U(s)$. Then if a play of the game results in a win for IN by generating an x in A, x will belong to some $U(s)$ included in A. But it takes only finitely many rounds of picks by the two players to generate s, and that means that by some finite stage IN will have, in effect, already won. Now suppose there is no winning strategy for IN. Call a position after finitely many rounds in the game *good* for OUT if IN still does not have a winning strategy for the continuation of the game from that point. If a position is good, then whatever IN picks next, there is some pick for OUT that would keep the position good. (Otherwise, IN could make a pick i for which this is not so, and whatever pick OUT then made, IN would have a strategy for the rest of the game, meaning that IN in effect had a winning strategy *already*, namely, to pick this i and follow up with the winning strategy associated with OUT's next pick.) Therefore OUT can always make a pick that will keep the position good, so at no finite stage will IN have won, meaning that IN will not win in the end, either. Always picking to keep the position good is a winning strategy for OUT.

David Blackwell, in a modest but insightful communication of 1967, pointed out how this theorem could be used to give a new game-theoretic proof of a classical structural theorem, the Kuratowski reduction principle for coanalytic sets. A flurry of intense activity led a decade or so later to the beautiful picture in Moschovakis (2009): PD implies not only all the regularity theorems but also all the structural theorems that the classical descriptive set theorists of the 1920s and 1930s were seeking but could not find because they are not provable in ZFC. Great interest consequently attaches to the question of how far one can go beyond the Gale–Stewart theorem within ZFC, and what plausible additional assumptions might take one all the way to PD.

There were partial results on low-level Borel sets by Morton Davis and others, and then D. A. Martin proved the determinateness of analytic and coanalytic sets *assuming a measurable cardinal*. He later proved in ZFC the determinateness of all Borel sets. Martin (2020) is a recent recounting of both results. Between Martin's two landmarks, Friedman (1971) showed, on the one hand, that analytic and coanalytic determinacy could not have been obtained in ZFC alone, and that Borel determinacy would have to make use of essentially the full strength of ZFC, and involve cardinals that, although not "large" by set theorists' standards, are much larger than any ordinarily encountered in mainstream mathematics. Later Woodin, and definitively Martin and John Steel (1989), showed that enough really *large* large cardinals – more specifically, enough Woodin cardinals – give PD. Just as there are results about the finite whose proofs take a detour through the infinite (as discussed in §8.3), so also there are results about the "lower" infinite, the realm of reals and sets of reals, whose proofs depend on the "higher" infinite, or realm of large cardinals.

Unfortunately, although large cardinals in this way have cleared up almost all outstanding problems about special sets of reals, in contrast to their thus telling us "everything" about descriptive set theory, they in themselves tell us almost nothing about CH, disappointing the expectations of Gödel, for one. For if a model *M* has in it an ordinal that appears to it to be a large cardinal, then it will still appear to be so after forcing involving any partial order *P* that appears to the model of smaller cardinality that that. And this includes the forcing "conditions" that can turn CH off or on. This was shown by Levy, Solovay, and others – it has to be proved anew for each type of large cardinal – in the early days of the reception of Cohen's work. Hence a continuing search on the part of set theorists for other candidate new axioms to prove or disprove CH, with MM being one example.

10.3 Large Cardinals and Inner Models

Scott (1961) discovered an important break in the series of stronger and stronger large cardinal axioms. The weaker ones, such as the existence of inaccessibles and the existence of weakly compacts, are compatible with $V = L$: if LC is either of these axioms, then $\mathrm{Con}(\mathrm{ZFC} + \mathrm{LC})$ implies $\mathrm{Con}(\mathrm{ZFC} + \mathrm{LC} + V = L)$. Thus "inaccessibles and weakly compacts can exist in L." But Scott showed that measurables cannot. (The measurable cardinal κ is present in L, since all ordinals are, but not its measure μ, so L does not "know" κ is measurable.). But Kunen (1970) showed there exists an L-*like* minimalistic model associated with $\mathrm{ZFC} + \mathrm{MC}$, where MC is the existence of measurable cardinals, which as he and subsequent workers established, shares many of the properties of the original L, with CH being true in it, in particular. This discovery launched the *inner model program*, to find L-like models for larger and larger cardinals, and analyze their fine structures. The program has since made considerable progress, the main outstanding case being super-compacts. Woodin, pursuing this line of thought, has been led to a vision of an "ultimate L" and an hypotheses that would among other things accommodate all large cardinals (bar Reinhardt), and imply $c = \aleph_1$.

Woodin's current leaning in this direction contrasts with an earlier leaning in the direction of a different hypothesis he called $(*)$ or "star" on account of the illumination it would cast on many problems, one of whose implications would be $c = \aleph_2$. It is rather rare for any paper in set theory to appear in the *Annals of Mathematics*, generally accounted the leading journal in the field, but while the present work was in preparation there appeared there a paper of David Asperó and Ralf Schindler (2021) proving that a souped-up variant of MM implies $(*)$, thus uniting two lines of work leading to the same conclusion about the value of c. This result has been found so newsworthy that journalistic popularizations have appeared, which, while avoiding technicalities, attempt to convey something of the spirit of the work through a mix of pictures, metaphors, and quotations attributed to experts. See Wachover (2021).

11 Concluding Philosophical Remarks

The *methodological problem* faced by set theorists concerns what to do about central set-theoretic questions such as CH whose status cannot be settled on the basis of the axioms generally accepted by the mathematical community, those of

ZFC. Here *optimists* hold that additional axioms that settle such questions can be, or perhaps already have been, found that can be justified in a way that is in some sense objective, either intrinsically by claiming that they really were implicit in our concept of set all along, or extrinsically in terms of the wealth and plausibility and utility of their consequences. By contrast, *pessimists* suspect we may have to acknowledge a bifurcation in the concept of set into a pair of distinct concepts, one leading to $c = \aleph_1$, one leading to $c = \aleph_2$ (a view sometimes compared to the Einsteinian bifurcation of the Newtonian notion of *mass* into *rest mass* and *inertial mass*, which makes some statements about "mass" true in one sense but false in another); or even worse, we may have to abandon altogether any attempt to settle such questions as the status of CH or SH, and so on, and embrace a "multiverse" of set-theoretic universes in different ones of which different combinations of such hypotheses hold, tracing out their interconnections (a view reminiscent of the speculations of those cosmologists who believe in a "multiverse" of different physical universes in which physical constants may have different values). There are also mathematicians unfriendly to set theory who hold that ZFC is already more than is needed to accommodate all really important core mathematics, and that speculations about abstruse set-theoretic issues going beyond this basic core should not be encouraged.

The *ontological problem* raised by metaphysicians less interested in the internal workings of a discipline like set theory than in its external relations, so to speak, and especially in the relation of its objects to those of physical science, is this: Are abstract entities – of which sets would be a prime example – utlimately real, or merely useful fictions? Metaphysical or ontological *realists* opt for the former, and *nominalists* for the latter alternative. There are also philosophers unfriendly to ontological metaphysics who question the intelligibility of talk of "ultimate reality."

Although authors of Elements are permitted, and even almost encouraged, to be opinionated, I do not wish to take a stand on either question here. Obviously, since I have undertaken to write the present work, I do not share the anti-set-theoretic stance (while nonetheless finding great interest in questions about how much set theory this or that kind of mathematics indispensably requires and how much it can get by without), but I disclaim any qualifications to speak on optimism *versus* pessimism. I am firmly antimetaphysical or anti-ontological in outlook, but I have expressed my views on that issue as well as I can elsewhere, and it is, in any case an issue that has more to do with mathematics in general than set theory in particular, which is my present subject.

What I think it important to emphasize about the optimism *versus* pessimism and the realism *versus* nominalism debates before closing here is simply their *distinctness*. Philosophy is not like sciences where international bodies regulate the use of terminology (the names of chemical compounds or of biological species, for instance), and as a result one finds a philosophical label such as "platonist" bandied about rather loosely, sometimes applied to set-theoretic optimists, sometimes applied to metaphysical realists. This kind of sloppiness can sow confusion, and so though warnings against conflating orthogonal issues have repeatedly been urged by Maddy and others, one more repetition of such cautions may be in order.

Let it be noted, therefore, first, that even in connection with a body of admitted pure fiction, say the canon of Sherlock Holmes stories of Conan Doyle, when presented with two continuations, say pastiches by two different subsequent writers, there are often objective (or anyhow, not wholly subjective) reasons for thinking one rather than the other more in harmony with the spirit of the original, and more worthy of being admitted as deuterocanonical rather than dismissed as apocryphal. In the same way, one could hold that "ultimate L" is, in some sense, objectively preferable to "Martin's maximum," or the reverse, while remaining doubtful whether in the end set theory is more than a grand mythology.

Let it be noted, also, second, that even in connection with physical objects whose reality no sane person doubts, there can be many questions about them that it is beyond our powers to answer. (A stock example is: What did Julius Caesar have for his last meal before he was assassinated?) There may even be deep reasons of physical principle (connected with the second law of thermo-dynamics) why there must be many such unanswerable physical questions. In the same way, one could be a firm believer in the absolute, fundamental, noumenal reality of the objects of set theory, while holding that many of their properties are entirely and forever beyond the range of human cognitive faculties.

Set theory is a grand subject, whether or not its oldest and deepest questions can ever be answered objectively, and whether it is in the end regarded as a revelation of an ultimate reality or as a purely human construction.

References

Asperó, D. & Schindler, R. (2021). Martin's Maximum^{++} Implies Woodin's Axiom (*), *Annals of Mathematic 193*, 793–835.

Barwise, J. (ed.) (1977). *Handbook of Mathematical Logic*, Amsterdam: North Holland.

Benacerraf, P. (1965). What Numbers Could Not Be, *Philosophical Review 74*, 47–73. Reprinted in Benacerraf, P. & Putnam, H. (eds.) (1983). *Philosophy of Mathematics: Selected Readings*, 2nd ed., Englewood Cliffs: Prentice Hall (pp. 272–94).

Benacerraf, P. & Putnam, H. (eds.) (1983). *Philosophy of Mathematics: Selected Readings*, 2nd ed., Englewood Cliffs: Prentice Hall.

Blackwell, D. (1967). Infinite Games and Analytic Sets, *Proceedings of the National Academy of Sciences 58*, 1836–7.

Blumenthal, L. M. (1940). A Paradox, a Paradox, a Most Ingenious Paradox, *American Mathematical Monthly 47*, 346–53.

Boole, G. (1854). *An Investigation of the Laws of Thought*, London: Macmillan.

Boolos, G. S. (1971). The Iterative Conception of Set, *Journal of Philosophy 68*, 215–31. Reprinted in Benacerraf, P. & Putnam, H. (eds.) (1983). *Philosophy of Mathematics: Selected Readings*, 2nd ed., Englewood Cliffs: Prentice Hall (pp. 486–502).

Boolos, G. S., Burgess, J. P., & Jeffrey, R. C. (2002). *Computability and Logic*, 5th ed., Cambridge: Cambridge University Press.

Bourbaki, N. [collective pseud.] (1939). *Théorie d'Ensembles: Fascicule de Résultats [Set Theory: Booklet of Results]*, Paris: Hermann.

Burgess, J. P. (1977). Forcing. In Barwise, J. (ed.) (1977). *Handbook of Mathematical Logic*, Amsterdam: North Holland (pp. 403–52).

Cantor, G. (1915). *Contributions to the Founding of the Theory of Transfinite Numbers*, tr. Jourdain, P. E. B., Chicago: Open Court.

Cohen, P. J. (1966). *Set Theory and the Continuum Hypothesis*, New York: W. A. Benjamin.

Davis, M. (1964). Infinite Games of Perfect Information, *Annals of Mathematical Studies 52*, Princeton: Princeton University Press.

Dedekind, R. (1901). *Essays on the Theory of Numbers*, tr. Beman, W. W., Chicago: Open Court.

Devlin, K. (1977). Constructibility. In Barwise, J. (ed.) (1977). *Handbook of Mathematical Logic*, Amsterdam: North Holland (pp. 453–90).

Erdös, P. & Tarski, A. (1961). On Some Problems Involving Inaccessible Cardinals,

Feferman, S., Dawson, J., & Kleene, S. (eds.) (1990). *Kurt Gödel: Collected Works II*, Oxford: Oxford University Press.

Fraenkel, A. (1922/1967). The Notion of "Definite" and the Independence of the Axiom of Choice, tr. Woodward, B. In van Heijenoort, J. (1967). *From Frege to Gödel: A Source Book in Mathematical Logic 1879–1931*, Cambridge, MA: Harvard University Press. (pp. 284–9).

Frege, G. (1879/1967). *Begriffsschrift*: A Formula Language Modeled on That of Arithmetic, for Pure Thought, tr. Bauer-Mengelberg, S. In van Heijenoort, J. (1967). *From Frege to Gödel: A Source Book in Mathematical Logic 1879–1931*, Cambridge, MA: Harvard University Press (pp. 1–82).

Frege, G. (1893). *Grundgesetze der Arithmetik I [Basic Laws of Arithmetic I]*, Jena: Hermann Pohle.

Friedman, H. (1971). Higher Set Theory and Mathematical Practice, *Annals of Mathematical Logic 2*, 325–57.

Gillman, L. (2002). Two Classical Surprises Concerning the Axiom of Choice and the Continuum Hypothesis, *American Mathematical Monthly 109*, 544–53.

Gödel, K. (1940). *The Consistency of the Continuum Hypothesis, Annals of Mathematical Studies 3*, Princeton: Princeton University Press.

Gödel, K. (1946/1965). Remarks before the Princeton Bicentennial Conference on Problems in Mathematics. In Davis, M. (ed.) (1965). *The Undecidable; Basic Papers on Undecidable Propositions, Unsolvable Problems and Computable Functions*, Hewlett: Raven Press (pp. 84–8). Reprinted in Feferman, S., Dawson, J., & Kleene, S. (eds.) (1990). *Kurt Gödel: Collected Works II*, Oxford: Oxford University Press (pp. 150–3).

Gödel, K. (1947). What Is Cantor's Continuum Problem? *American Mathematical Monthly 9*, 515–25. Reprinted with modifications in Benacerraf, P. & Putnam, H. (eds.) (1983). *Philosophy of Mathematics: Selected Readings*, 2nd ed., Englewood Cliffs: Prentice Hall (pp. 470–85), and in both original and modified versions in Feferman, S., Dawson, J., & Kleene, S. (eds.) (1990). *Kurt Gödel: Collected Works II*, Oxford: Oxford University Press (pp. 154–84).

Halmos, P. (1960). *Naive Set Theory*, Princeton: Van Nostrand.

Hamilton, W. R. (1853). *Lectures on Quaternions*, Dublin: Hodges & Smith.

Hardy, G. H. (1914). *A Course of Pure Mathematics*, 2nd ed., Cambridge: Cambridge University Press.

Hartogs, F. (1915). Über das Problem der Wohlordnung [On the Problem of Wellordering], *Mathematische Annalen 36*, 438–43.

Holmes, R. (2014). Alternative Axiomatic Set Theories, *Stanford Encyclopedia of Philosophy*, plato.stanford.edu/archives/fall2014/entries/settheory-alternative/.

Hrbacek, K. & Jech, T. (1999). *Introduction to Set Theory: Revised and Expanded*, 3rd ed., New York: Marcel Dekker.

Incurvati, L. (2020). *Conceptions of Sets and Foundations of Mathematics*, Cambridge: Cambridge University Press.

Kanamori, A. (2003). *The Higher Infinite, Large Cardinals in Set Theory from Their Beginnings*, Berlin, Springer.

Kanamori, A. (2010) (ed.). Introduction. In Foreman, M. & Kanamori, A. (eds.). *Handbook of Set Theory I*, Berlin: Springer (pp. 1–92).

Koellner, P. (2009). On Reflection Principles, *Annals of Pure and Applied Logic 157*, 206–19.

Kunen, K. (1970). Some Applications of Iterated Ultrapowers in Set Theory, *Annals of Mathematical Logic 1*, 179–227.

Kunen, K. (1977). Combinatorics. In Barwise, J. (ed.) (1977). *Handbook of Mathematical Logic*, Amsterdam: North Holland (pp. 371–402).

Kuratowski, K. (1966). *Topologys*, Warsaw: Polish Scientific Publishers.

Landau, E. (1930). *Foundations of Analysis: The Arithmetic of Whole, Rational, Irrational, and Complex Numbers*, tr. Steinhardt, F., Providence: Chelsea.

Lebesgue, H. (1902). *Intégrale, Longueur, Aire [Integral, Length, Area]*, Milan: Bernardoni & Rebeschini.

Levy, A. (1960). Axiom Schemata of Strong Infinity in Axiomatic Set Theory, *Pacific Journal of Mathematics 10*, 223–38.

Maddy, P. (2011). *Defending the Axioms*, Oxford: Oxford University Press.

Maddy, P. (2017). Set-Theoretic Foundations. In Caicedo, A. E. (ed.). *Foundations of Mathematics: Essays in Honor of W. Hugh Woodin's 60th Birthday*, Providence: American Mathematical Society (pp. 289–322).

Martin, D. A. (2020) *Determinacy of Infinitely Long Games* (preprint). www.math.ucla.edu/~dam/booketc/thebook.pdf.

Martin, D. A. & Solovay, R. (1970). Internal Cohen Extensions, *Annals of Mathematical Logic 2*, 143–78.

Martin, D. A. & Steel, J. R. (1989). A Proof of Projective Determinacy, *Journal of the American Mathematical Society 2*, 71–125.

Mathias, A. R. D. (1992). What Is Mac Lane Missing? In Judah, H., Just, W., & Woodin, H. *Set Theory and the Continuum*, Mathematical Sciences Research Institute Publications 26, Berlin: Springer.

Moschovakis, Y. (2009) *Descriptive Set Theory*, 2nd ed., Providence: American Mathematical Society.

Poincaré, H. (1905/1983). On the Nature of Mathematical Reasoning, tr. W. J. G. [initials only indicated], in Benacerraf, P. & Putnam, H. (eds.) (1983). *Philosophy of Mathematics: Selected Readings*, 2nd ed., Englewood Cliffs: Prentice Hall (pp. 377–93).

Putnam, H. (1980). Models and Reality. *Journal of Symbolic Logic 45*, 464–82. Reprinted in Benacerraf, P. & Putnam. H. (eds.) *Philosophy of Mathematics: Selected Readings*, 2nd ed., Englewood Cliffs: Prentice Hall (1983) (pp. 421–46).

Ramsey, F. P. (1925) The Foundations of Mathematics, *Proceedings of the London Mathematical Society 25*, 338–84.

Ramsey, F. P. (1930) On a Problem of Formal Logic, *Proceedings of the London Mathematical Society 30*, 264–86.

Rubin, H. & Rubin, J. E. (1970). *Equivalents of the Axiom of Choice II*, Amsterdam: North Holland.

Rudin, M. E. (1977). Martin's Axiom. In Barwise, J. (ed.) (1977). *Handbook of Mathematical Logic*, Amsterdam: North Holland (pp. 491–502).

Russell, B. (1902). Letter to Frege. In van Heijenoort, J. (1967). *From Frege to Gödel: A Source Book in Mathematical Logic 1879–1931*, Cambridge, MA: Harvard University Press (pp. 124–5).

Russell, B. (1908). Mathematical Logic as Based on the Theory of Types, *American Journal of Mathematics 30*, 222–62. Reprinted in van Heijenoort, J. (1967). *From Frege to Gödel: A Source Book in Mathematical Logic 1879–1931,* Cambridge, MA: Harvard University Press (pp. 153–82).

Scott, D. (1961). Measurable Cardinals and Constructible Sets. *Bulletin de l'Académie Polonaise des Sciences*, Série des sciences mathématiques, astronomiques et physiques *9*, 521–4.

Sierpinski, W. (1956). *L'Hypothèse du Continu* [*The Continuum Hypothesis*], Providence: Chelsea.

Sierpinski, W. (1958). *Cardinal and Ordinal Numbers*, Warsaw: Polish Scientific Publishers.

Skolem, T. (1922/1967). Some Remarks on Axiomatic Set Theory, tr. Bauer-Mengelberg, S. In van Heijenoort, J. (1967). *From Frege to Gödel: A Source Book in Mathematical Logic 1879–1931*, Cambridge, MA: Harvard University Press (pp. 290–301).

Tarski, A. & Vaught, R. L. (1956) Arithmetical Extensions of Relational Systems, *Compositio Mathematica 13*, 81–102.

van Heijenoort, J. (1967). *From Frege to Gödel: A Source Book in Mathematical Logic 1879–1931*, Cambridge, MA: Harvard University Press.

Vitali, G. (1905). *Sulla Problema della Mesura dei Gruppi di Punti di una Retta* [*On the Problem of the Measure of Sets of Points on a Line*], Bologna: Gamberini & Parmeggiani.

von Neumann, J. (1923/1967). On the Introduction of Transfinite Numbers, tr. Bauer-Mengelberg, S. In van Heijenoort, J. (1967). *From Frege to Gödel: A Source Book in Mathematical Logic 1879–1931*, Cambridge, MA: Harvard University Press (pp. 346–54).

Wachover, N. (2021). How Many Numbers Exist? Infinite Proof Moves Math Closer to an Answer, *Quanta Magazine*. www.quantamagazine.org/how-many-numbers-exist-infinity-proof-moves-math-closer-to-an-answer-20210715/.

Whitehead, A. N. & Russell, B. (1910). *Principia Mathematical I*, Cambridge: Cambridge University Press.

Zermelo, E. (1908/1967). Investigations in the Foundations of Set Theory I, tr. Bauer-Mengelberg, S. In van Heijenoort, J. (1967). *From Frege to Gödel: A Source Book in Mathematical Logic 1879–1931*, Cambridge, MA: Harvard University Press (pp. 199–215).

Zermelo, E. (1930). Über Grenzzahlen und Mengenbereiche: Neue Untersuchungen über die Grundlagen der Mengenlehre [On Boundary-Numbers and Set-Domains: New Investigations in the Foundations of Set Theory], *Fundamenta Mathematicae 16*, 29–47.

Acknowledgments

This work was written after more than fifty years of study, research, and teaching in set theory, during which the author has accumulated debts of gratitude to more individuals than can be mentioned. But I would especially like to acknowledge the influence, on the one hand, during my years as a graduate student at Berkeley in the early 1970s, of my teachers Ronald Jensen, Ashok Maitra, Jack Silver, Robert Solovay, and Robert Vaught, and, on the other hand, then and later, of my fellow students at the time, Penelope Maddy, Douglas Miller, and Lee Stanley. I would also like to mention with gratitude the small but engaged group of Princeton undergraduates who were studying the subject with me as I worked on the manuscript of the present work during the difficult era of COVID-19: Yamaan Attwa, Felipe Doria, Zander Hill, Jake Intrater, Tanvi Kishore, Noah Luch, Max Manicone, Sam Mathers, and Elijah Shina. The work is dedicated to Ruby Eloise Burgess and Stella Rose Burgess.

Cambridge Elements

Philosophy and Logic

Bradley Armour-Garb
SUNY Albany

Brad Armour-Garb is chair and Professor of Philosophy at SUNY Albany. His books include *The Law of Non-Contradiction* (coedited with Graham Priest and J. C. Beall, 2004), *Deflationary Truth* and *Deflationism and Paradox* (both coedited with J. C. Beall, 2005), *Pretense and Pathology* (with James Woodbridge, Cambridge University Press, 2015), *Reflections on the Liar* (2017), and *Fictionalism in Philosophy* (coedited with Fred Kroon, 2020).

Frederick Kroon
The University of Auckland

Frederick Kroon is Emeritus Professor of Philosophy at the University of Auckland. He has authored numerous papers in formal and philosophical logic, ethics, philosophy of language, and metaphysics, and is the author of *A Critical Introduction to Fictionalism* (with Stuart Brock and Jonathan McKeown-Green, 2018).

About the Series

This Cambridge Elements series provides an extensive overview of the many and varied connections between philosophy and logic. Distinguished authors provide an up-to-date summary of the results of current research in their fields and give their own take on what they believe are the most significant debates influencing research, drawing original conclusions.

Cambridge Elements $^{\equiv}$

Philosophy and Logic

Printed in the United States
by Baker & Taylor Publisher Services